WORLD BANK TECHNICAL PAPER NO. 496

Design and Appraisal of Rural Transport Infrastructure

Ensuring Basic Access for Rural Communities

Jerry Lebo
Dieter Schelling

The World Bank
Washington, D.C.

Copyright © 2001
The International Bank for Reconstruction
and Development/THE WORLD BANK
1818 H Street, N.W.
Washington, D.C. 20433, U.S.A.

All rights reserved
Manufactured in the United States of America
First printing April 2001
1 2 3 4 04 03 02 01

Technical Papers are published to communicate the results of the Bank's work to the development community with the least possible delay. The typescript of this paper therefore has not been prepared in accordance with the procedures appropriate to formal printed texts, and the World Bank accepts no responsibility for errors. Some sources cited in this paper may be informal documents that are not readily available.

The findings, interpretations, and conclusions expressed in this paper are entirely those of the author(s) and should not be attributed in any manner to the World Bank, to its affiliated organizations, or to members of its Board of Executive Directors or the countries they represent. The World Bank does not guarantee the accuracy of the data included in this publication and accepts no responsibility for any consequence of their use. The boundaries, colors, denominations, and other information shown on any map in this volume do not imply on the part of the World Bank Group any judgment on the legal status of any territory or the endorsement or acceptance of such boundaries.

The material in this publication is copyrighted. The World Bank encourages dissemination of its work and will normally grant permission promptly.

Permission to photocopy items for internal or personal use, for the internal or personal use of specific clients, or for educational classroom use, is granted by the World Bank, provided that the appropriate fee is paid directly to Copyright Clearance Center, Inc., 222 Rosewood Drive, Danvers, MA 01923, U.S.A., telephone 978-750-8400, fax 978-750-4470. Please contact the Copyright Clearance Center before photocopying items.

For permission to reprint individual articles or chapters, please fax your request with complete information to the Republication Department, Copyright Clearance Center, fax 978-750-4470.

All other queries on rights and licenses should be addressed to the World Bank at the address above or faxed to 202-522-2422.

ISBN: 0-8213-4919-8
ISSN: 0253-7494

Jerry Lebo is a senior transport specialist in the Transport and Urban Development Department at the World Bank. Dieter Schelling is a lead rural transport specialist in the Africa Regional Office of the World Bank.

Library of Congress Cataloging-in-Publication Data has been applied for.

CONTENTS

Foreword iv

Abstract v

Acknowledgments vi

Acronyms and Abbreviations vii

Overview and Conclusions 1
    Rural Transport Infrastructure and Poverty Alleviation 1
    The Concept of Basic Access 1
    Designing Rural Transport Infrastructure for Basic Access 2
    Appraising Rural Transport Infrastructure for Basic Access 2
    Conclusions 3

1. Introduction 4
    The Rationale for Action 4
    Structure and Context 5

2. Concepts and Definitions 6
    Rural Transport and Poverty Reduction Strategies 6
    A Holistic Approach to Rural Transport 6
    What is Rural Transport Infrastructure? 8
    A Basic Access Approach to RTI Investments 9

3. Designing RTI for Basic Access 11
    Access and "Level of Service" 11
    Basic Access 12
    Engineering Design of Basic Access RTI 16
    Implementation Methods 18
    Maintenance of Basic Access RTI 20

4. Appraising RTI for Basic Access 21
    A Participatory Planning Approach 21
    Selection and Priority Setting Methods 24
    Multi-Criteria Analysis 25
    Cost-Effectiveness Analysis 25
    Cost-Benefit Analysis 28
    Extending the CBA Framework for RTI 29

Appendix A: Road Network, Mobility and Accessibility in Selected Countries 34

Appendix B: Designing Basic Access Roads 35

Appendix C: Designing Basic Access RTI for Non-motorized Means of Transport 59

Appendix D: Low-cost Traffic Survey Methods for RTI 65

Appendix E: Samples of Innovative Economic Appraisals of RTI Investments 68

Appendix F: Low Volume Roads Economic Decision Model (RED) 80

Notes 83

Bibliography 91

FOREWORD

The purpose of this paper is to assist rural transport planners, rural road agencies, donor agencies, local governments, and communities in the design and appraisal of rural transport infrastructure (RTI) interventions. It especially focuses on how RTI can contribute to poverty reduction. *Design and Appraisal of Rural Transport Infrastructure* appears as part of a four-volume compendium of rural transport knowledge under development by the World Bank's Rural Transport Thematic Group. The other three publications are *Options for the Managing and Financing of Rural Transport Infrastructure*, published in 1998,[1] *Improving Rural Mobility*, and *Developing Rural Transport Policies and Strategies*.[2]

The poor condition of rural transport networks in many developing countries blocks poverty-reduction efforts and stifles economic growth. A period of government and donor focus on the management and financing of main road networks is beginning to yield increased institutional and financial capacity, as well as improved main roads. Coupled with the clear emphasis on poverty reduction, this has led developing countries and the donor community to show new interest in building sustainable rural transport networks.

Meanwhile, a more holistic view of rural transport has emerged. Instead of narrowly focusing on roads, it takes into account the provision and affordability of transport services, intermediate means of transport, and the location and quality of services. The sustainable provision of rural transport networks (referred to as rural transport infrastructure, so as to include tracks, paths, and footbridges) crucially depends on appropriate management and financing arrangements, including a sound approach to design and appraisal.

This paper focuses on the design and appraisal of rural transport infrastructure. The task is especially urgent considering evidence that developing countries often adopt excessively high standards of access, particularly when donor financing is involved. Given scarce resources, such an approach raises long-term maintenance costs and denies access to underserved populations. Instead, a *basic access approach* is recommended, whereby priority is given to the provision of reliable, least-cost, all-season basic access to as many people as possible.

For some time now, it has been clear that rural transport infrastructure is ill-suited for appraisal using the conventional economic cost-benefit analysis, as it is applied to highly trafficked main roads. Rather, a wider view is needed to assess the role of low-volume transport infrastructure interventions, including the social importance of ensuring a minimal level of access to resources and opportunities. Examples of economic appraisals applied in recent World Bank rural transport projects illustrate this approach.

John Flora
Director
Transport
Urban Development

ABSTRACT

Isolation contributes to rural poverty. Without a minimum of reliable and efficient access to locations of basic social and economic activities, rural life stagnates and local development prospects remain limited. Providing and maintaining a minimum level of access, referred to in this paper as basic access, is therefore a necessary element of any rural development strategy.

Overcoming isolation necessitates holistic strategies. Approaches include improved logistics to support trade and communication, the promotion of transport services and intermediate means of transport, improved quality and location of services, and the sustainable provision of cost-effective transport infrastructure. Among these, the cost-effective design and appraisal of rural transport infrastructure (RTI) is the topic of this paper.

A basic access approach to the provision of RTI is presented which gives priority to the provision and maintenance of reliable, all-season access. Basic access interventions are defined as the least-cost investments which provide a minimum level of all-season passability. In a majority of cases, this means single-lane, spot-improved earth or gravel roads. In situations where motorized basic access is not affordable, improvement of the existing path network and the construction of footbridges may be the only alternative.

Resources are scarce. Therefore the basic access approach should only employ the most appropriate and cost-effective interventions. In this context, participatory selection procedures and analytical prioritization tools are presented, and examples given, which take into account the social and economic importance of RTI.

ACKNOWLEDGMENTS

This paper is a collaborative effort of the World Bank's Rural Transport Thematic Group and partners and experts from the global rural transport community. It was prepared by Jerry Lebo and Dieter Schelling of the Transport Department (INFTD) within the Private Sector Development and Infrastructure Vice Presidency of the World Bank Group. Financing was provided by the Swiss Government and the World Bank..

Particular contributions to the design aspects of the paper were made by David Stiedl, Andreas Beusch, Arnaud Desmarchelier, and Sally Burningham. Alan Ross made valuable contributions on road safety, as did Sonia Kapoor for environmental impact mitigation. Thampil Pankaj, Rodrigo Archondo-Callao, Liu Zhi and Colin Gannon were major contributors to the appraisal aspects of the paper. Walter Osterwalder contributed both the cover photograph and valuable comments.

Valuable feedback at various stages was provided by experts from the international rural transport community including, John Howe, Collins Makoriwa, Peter Roberts, John Hine, Simon Ellis, Setty Pendakur, Richard Robinson, Peter Winkelmann, Fatemeh Ali-Nejadfard, Terje Tessem, Jane Tournee and Margaret Grieco.

A number of colleagues at the Bank provided important feedback: Moctar Thiam, Susanne Holste, Andreas Schliessler, Hatim Hajj, Louis Pouliquen, Paul Guitink, Subhash Seth and Henri Beenhakker.

We are especially grateful for the extremely useful in-depth comments and reviews provided by Christina Malmberg Calvo, Juan Gaviria, John Riverson and George Banjo.

The publication was edited by Steve Dorst of Dorst Mediaworks and formatted by Barbara Gregory and Tipawan Bhutaprateep.

ACRONYMS AND ABBREVIATIONS

AC	Asphalt Concrete
ADT	Average Daily Traffic
CBA	Cost-Benefit Analysis
CBR	California Bearing Ratio
CEA	Cost-Effectiveness Analysis
EA	Environmental Assessment
ERR	Economic Rate of Return
EMAP	Environmental Management Action Plan
HDM-4	Highway Development and Management Model – Version 4
IFRTD	International Forum for Rural Transport and Development
IMT	Intermediate Means of Transport
LGR	Local Government Road
MCA	Multi-Criteria Analysis
MOC	Moving Observer Count
MTS	Manual Traffic Survey
NMT	Non-Motorized Means of Transport
NPV	Net Present Value
PAD	Project Appraisal Document
PCU	Passenger Car Unit
RAP	Resettlement Action Plan
RED	Road Economic Decision Model
RT	Rural Transport
RTI	Rural Transport Infrastructure
RTS	Rural Transport Services
RTTP	Rural Travel and Transport Program
SA	Social Assessment
SD	Surface Dressing
SP	Shrinkage Product
SSATP	Sub-Saharan African Transport Policy Program
TOR	Terms of Reference
TRL	Transport Research Laboratory, UK
VPD	Motorized, four-wheeled Vehicles Per Day
VOC	Vehicle Operating Costs
WB	World Bank
$	United States Dollar

OVERVIEW AND CONCLUSIONS

Rural transport networks in most developing countries are underdeveloped and of poor quality. It is estimated that about 900 million rural dwellers in developing countries do not have reliable all-season access to main road networks, and about 300 million do not have motorized access at all. At the same time, resources are being spent on upgrading roads to higher than economically justified standards for populations that already have a reasonable level of access.

Rural Transport Infrastructure and Poverty Alleviation

Various studies have provided evidence that poverty is more pervasive in areas with no or unreliable (motorized) access—what are referred to as unconnected areas. For example, in Nepal, where the percentage of people below the poverty line is as high as 42 percent, the incidence of poverty in unconnected areas is 70 percent. In Bhutan, the enrollment of girls in primary schools is three times as high in connected villages compared to unconnected ones. In Andhra Pradesh, India, the female literacy rate is 60 percent higher in villages with all-season road access compared to those with unreliable access.

There is a growing body of evidence that rural transport infrastructure (RTI) is an essential, but not sufficient, ingredient of rural development and sustained poverty reduction. Additional building blocks for rural development include complementary public and private investment, such as water and energy supply, productive activities, and social and economic services.

For rural transport interventions, a new approach is emerging which requires a more holistic understanding of the mobility and access needs of rural communities. The affected communities themselves are leading this demand-driven, participatory approach. In this context, rural transport consists of three elements: (a) transport services, (b) location and quality of facilities, and (c) transport infrastructure. This approach acknowledges that intervention may be required in all three categories, not simply the latter. To effectively utilize and target available resources, country specific rural transport policies and strategies are required.

The Concept of Basic Access

Basic access is the minimum level of RTI network service required to sustain socioeconomic activity. Accordingly, the provision of basic access is often viewed as a basic human right, similar to the provision of basic health and basic education. Consistent with a basic needs focus, the *basic access approach* gives priority to the provision of reliable, all-season access, to as many villages as possible, over the upgrading of individual links to higher than basic access standard. A basic access intervention, in this context, can be defined as the least-cost (in terms of total life-cycle cost) intervention for ensuring reliable, all-season passability for the locally prevailing means of transport.

In a particular context or country, the ability to provide basic access is limited by resources. A key questions, therefore, that must be posed: what is *affordable*? Resources for RTI are typically scarce, with very limited support from the central government or other external sources.[3] Affordability therefore will primarily be determined by a population's capacity to maintain their basic access infrastructure over the long term. In cases where motorized basic access is not affordable, improvements to the existing path network and the provision of footbridges may be the only affordable alternative.

Designing Rural Transport Infrastructure for Basic Access

The majority of RTI in developing countries carries traffic of less than 50 motorized four-wheeled vehicles per day (VPD), but often a substantial number of intermediate means of transport, such as bicycles and animal-drawn carts. In most cases, the appropriate standard for these are single-lane, spot-improved earth or gravel roads[4] provided with low-cost drainage structures, such as fords and submersible single-lane bridges.

The (trouble) spot improvement approach is the key to the least-cost design. Cost savings of 50 to 90 percent can be achieved compared with fully engineered roads of equal standard throughout. However, to put this approach into practice, a variety of constraints, such as political pressure and road agency and donor preference for high-standard, high-cost roads[5] need to be overcome. More recently, some donor-financed interventions, in close collaboration with the responsible road agencies, have successfully implemented projects based on the spot improvement approach.

Labor-based approaches are best-suited for the implementation of RTI interventions. By transferring financial resources and skills to the local level, labor-based strategies can have a substantial poverty-reducing impact. They also have the potential to improve the gender distribution of income, providing employment opportunities for women where wage-employment is scarce.

Appraising Rural Transport Infrastructure for Basic Access

Due to the increasingly decentralized framework for the provision of local services, and in order to build ownership and mobilize local resources, the planning (and monitoring and evaluation) process for RTI must be participatory. Whereas simultaneously "bottom-up" and "top-down" iterative approaches are required, the starting point for the process consists of consultations at the local government and community level.

A key tool for the participatory planning process is a local government or community transport plan. Local engineers or consultants, in consultation with communities, should conduct a low-cost inventory and condition survey of the local transport network, including roads, tracks, paths and footbridges, with a focus on existing obstacles. On the basis of the information generated, and additional economic, social and demographic information, an "as is" map should be produced. Based on such information, stakeholders can cooperatively decide upon desired improvements in the RTI network, taking into account objectives and available resources.

Establishing the priorities of an RTI intervention requires a selection process consisting of a combination of screening and ranking procedures. The screening process reduces the number of investment alternatives. This can be done, for example, through targeting of disadvantaged communities based on poverty indexes, or by eliminating low-priority links from the list according to agreed criteria. The balance of the alternatives will need to be ranked according to priority. Three methodologies for ranking are discussed: (a) multi-criteria analysis (MCA); (b) cost-effectiveness analysis (CEA); and (c) cost-benefit analysis (CBA). MCA often leads to non-transparent results, and is recommended only if cost criteria are included, and if the criteria are few, relevant, and have been determined (including their relative weights) in a participatory way.

This publication proposes a specific CEA approach for the majority of RTI where traffic is less than 50 motorized four-wheeled vehicles per day. A priority index is defined for each RTI link based on a cost-effectiveness indicator equal to the ratio of the total life-cycle cost necessary to ensure basic access, divided by the population served. With this approach, a threshold CE-value needs to be determined below which a link should not be considered for investment. The recommended method for determining a threshold CE-value is to do a sample cost-benefit analysis on a few selected links applying enhanced benefit measurement approaches for establishing a threshold CE-value.[6]

For roads where higher than basic access standards seem justified—for example, those that provide an alternative access to the same location, or experience traffic levels above 50 VPD (but below 200 VPD)—the use of standard cost-benefit analysis is recommended. Appropriate computer-assisted models exist to aid transport planners and road agencies to optimize decisions on, among others, the threshold traffic for upgrading to a higher standard gravel or bituminous surface road. Such models include enhanced CBA and RED (Box 4.4). For roads that carry above 200 VPD, the utilization of HDM-4 is recommended.

Conclusions

In order to complement poverty reduction strategies, rural transport interventions must be an integral part of rural development interventions and focus on the mobility and access needs of rural communities. Substantial gains in accessibility—for more communities, in more regions of a country—are possible if rural transport infrastructure interventions are designed in a least-cost, network-based manner focusing on eliminating trouble spots. In view of budget constraints, selecting interventions requires a participatory physical planning process undertaken jointly with concerned local governments and communities, supported and coordinated by regional or central government agencies. Simple screening methods facilitate the selection process, reducing the number of alternatives to a manageable level. Ranking is then applied to the remaining options, and in most cases (below 50 VPD) the use of cost-effectiveness methods is recommended, supported by sample cost-benefit analysis on selected links, where appropriate.

1. INTRODUCTION

Three billion people in developing countries, or about two-thirds of their population, live in rural areas. The majority of them survive on less than two dollars a day, and about 1.2 billion live on less than a dollar a day.[7] Their lives are characterized by isolation, exclusion, and unreliable access to even the most basic economic opportunities and social services. For the majority of their transport needs, they rely on non-motorized means and on rugged paths, tracks and roads which are typically in poor condition and often only passable in dry weather.

For purposes of this paper, rural roads, tracks, paths and footbridges are referred to as rural transport infrastructure (RTI). The RTI network in developing countries consists of an estimated 5-6 million kilometers of designated[8] rural roads and an additional expansive network of undesignated roads, tracks, and paths. While the length of the undesignated network is unknown, it is estimated to be several times the extent of the designated network.[9] The vast majority of trips that take place over RTI (more than 80 percent) are short distances (less than five kilometers) and made by non-motorized means, including walking, animals, bicycle, and porterage.[10]

The Rationale for Action

Rural transport networks in most developing countries are still underdeveloped and of poor quality. Rural households, and particularly women, spend much time and effort on transport activities to fulfill their basic needs. Too many communities still do not have reliable access to main road networks or motorized access,[11] while at the same time resources are being spent upgrading roads to economically unjustified standards for populations that already have a sufficient level of access.

In recent years, renewed emphasis on assisting very poor populations through sustained rural development[12] has led governments and donors to accelerate resource flows to rural infrastructure, with a large proportion being directed at improving transport infrastructure. While these projects are sometimes sector-focused, they are increasingly taking the shape of multi-component rural development projects or social funds with an emphasis on local government and community-based program management. While a cross-sector orientation in such projects is desirable, there is a need for sound technical advice on the design of sub-components and, in particular, on appropriate design and appraisal methods for RTI.

Ensuring an effective RTI system is an essential requirement for rural development, although by itself, it is not sufficient to guarantee success. Without adequate RTI, communities lack the necessary physical access for basic domestic chores, agricultural activities, social and economic services and job opportunities. Without reliable access to markets and productive resources, economic development stagnates, and poverty reduction cannot be sustained. Improvements of the intra- and near-village path and track network, and the provision of all-season basic motorized access—if affordable and appropriate—are therefore essential conditions for rural development.

There is clear evidence that poverty is more pervasive in areas with no or unreliable (motorized access) as compared to more accessible areas. For example, in Nepal, where the percentage of people below the poverty line is as high as 42 percent, in unconnected areas 70 percent of people are living below the poverty line.[13] In Bhutan, the enrollment of girls in primary schools is three times as high in connected villages compared to unconnected ones.[14] In Andhra Pradesh, India, the female literacy rate is 60 percent higher in villages with all-season road access compared to those with unreliable access.[15] Plenty of further evidence of the socioeconomic impact of rural roads exists.[16]

Worldwide experience from past rural development programs and policies suggests that improving the poverty impact of RTI interventions requires attention to three guiding principles:[17]

- An emphasis on reliable, cost-effective access to as many of the rural population as possible, rather than high access standards for a few;

- Cost-effective and innovative techniques such as spot improvement, labor-based approaches, and low-cost structures, and;

- A decentralized and participatory approach with strong local government and community involvement in decision making on local transport investment and maintenance.

Consistent with this experience, this paper proposes approaches to the design and appraisal of rural transport infrastructure that emphasize innovative least-cost solutions for providing locally affordable basic access, as well as appropriate analytical tools and participatory methods for the selection of interventions.

Structure and Context

The paper is presented in four chapters. Chapter One introduces the topic. Chapter Two defines the terminology and concepts that will be used throughout the paper. Chapter Three explains the key elements of design for basic access transport infrastructure. Chapter Four gives guidance for selecting and prioritizing basic access-oriented interventions. Appendix A compares road network, mobility and accessibility indicators of selected countries. In Appendixes B and C, good practice examples are shown for basic access solutions to both motorized and non-motorized transport in a variety of geographic conditions. Appendix D presents low-cost traffic survey methods. Appendix E provides samples of innovative economic appraisals of RTI investments, and Appendix F describes the low volume Roads Economic Decision Model.

This paper is part of a four-volume series of publications on rural transport promoted by the World Bank's Rural Transport Thematic Group under the aegis of its knowledge management activities. The four volumes are: *Options for Managing and Financing Rural Transport Infrastructure, Improving Rural Mobility, Developing Rural Transport Policies and Strategies,* and this paper on *Design and Appraisal of Rural Transport Infrastructure*.[18]

2. CONCEPTS AND DEFINITIONS

Rural Transport and Poverty Reduction Strategies

Poverty reduction strategies require a comprehensive framework for implementation.[19] The simultaneous development of adequate rural infrastructure, productive sectors, social and economic services, an appropriate macroeconomic framework, and good governance and local ownership, is required for rural poverty alleviation (Figure 2.1 below). Effective transport, as a complementary input to nearly every aspect of rural activity, is an essential element of rural poverty reduction.

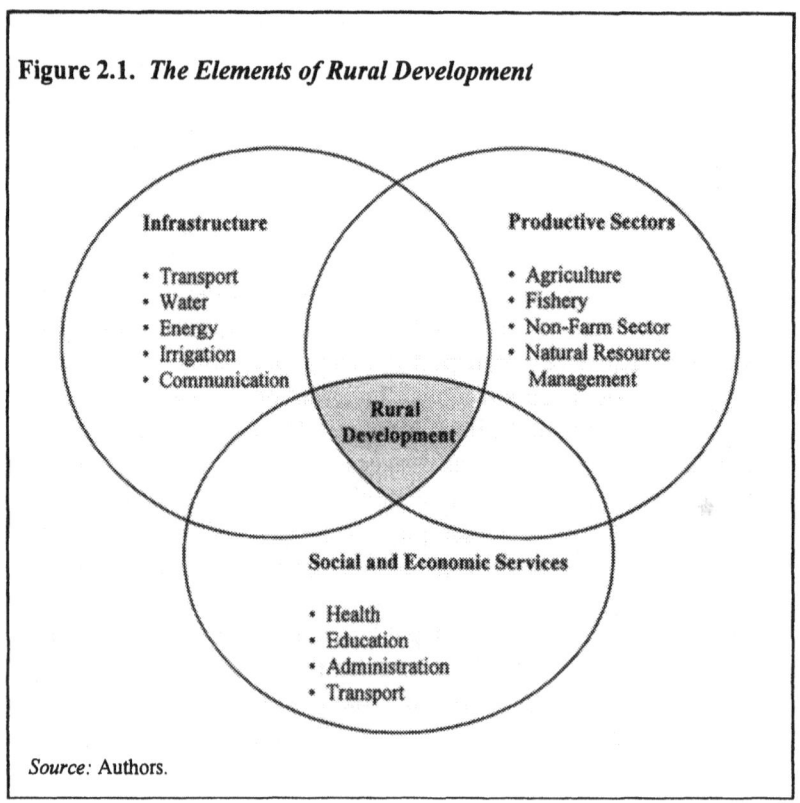

Figure 2.1. *The Elements of Rural Development*

Source: Authors.

A Holistic Approach to Rural Transport

A new approach to rural transport interventions is emerging. It requires a more holistic understanding of the mobility and access needs of the rural communities than has traditionally been the case in rural road sub-sector investments. It is a demand-led, or people-centered, approach with an emphasis on the needs expressed by affected communities. In this context, rural transport is more broadly seen as an input into successful rural livelihood strategies, within which access consists of three complementary elements: (a) means of transport, (b) location and quality of facilities, and (c) transport infrastructure. The approach acknowledges that intervention may be required in all three categories, not simply the latter (Figure 2.2).[20]

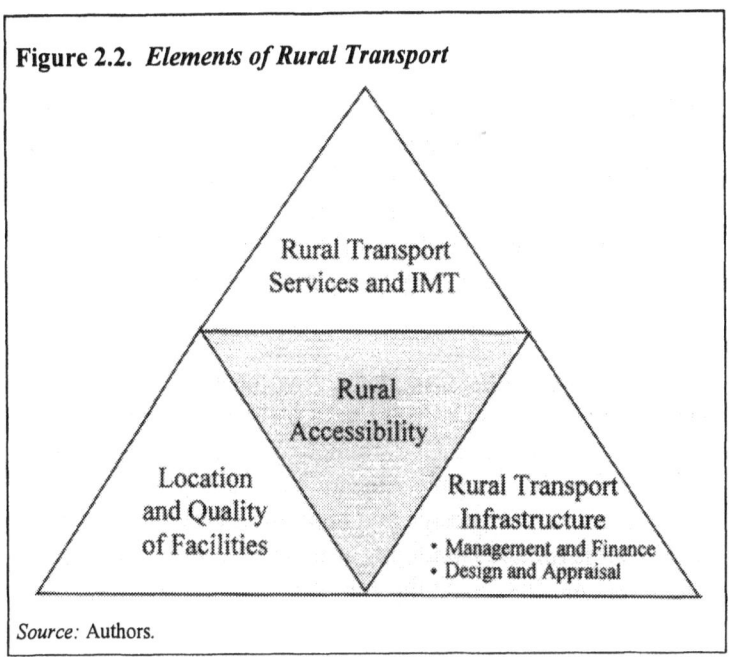

Figure 2.2. *Elements of Rural Transport*

Source: Authors.

Promoting Rural Transport Services (RTS) and Intermediate Means of Transport (IMT): [21] The availability and affordability of rural transport services and intermediate means of transport are crucial to rural development. The single pick-up truck that arrives once a week with essential supplies for the health center and school, as well as agricultural inputs, can be of immeasurable importance to a local community. Any investment program for improving RTI needs to carefully examine the constraints to effective RTS provision and to the ownership of IMT. Such constraints include excessive taxation, regulatory restrictions, inadequate markets, and the absence of credit facilities. Successful approaches to improving transport services must deal with issues related to low population density and transport demand in rural areas, should be cost-effective and use flexible technology.

Few poor rural dwellers own IMT such as bicycles and animal-drawn carts, let alone motorized means of transport. Most of the rural population walk and carry their loads, while the slightly better-off make use of IMT and RTS for the transportation of their products and themselves. For distances up to five kilometers, and even as far as 20 kilometers in some circumstances, walking is by far the most common mode of transportation in rural areas of developing countries.[22] Where RTS are provided, they usually consist of (a) privately provided transport services, often by pick-up trucks for both passengers and freight; and (b) for-hire non-motorized services such as bicycles, rickshaws, donkey carts, and so forth. Government extension services in the agriculture, health and education sectors may also provide informal transport services.

Location and Quality of Facilities: The second element of a comprehensive rural transport framework is the location and quality of facilities. The distance from households to facilities such as wells, forests, grinding mills, schools, and health centers determines the amount of time rural dwellers spend on transport activities. Numerous studies on rural transport have shown that rural households, and particularly women, spend a substantial amount of time and effort on transport activities.[23] The bulk of these efforts is required for domestic subsistence activities, particularly the collection of water and firewood, and trips to grinding mills. In the view of planners, this time is unproductive and wasted, and a drain on potentially productive labor—the principal economic resource for most rural households.[24] Therefore, improved quality and better locations of facilities are important to consider when examining alternative access improvements.[25]

Since the majority of time rural households spend on transport is for domestic activities, the most effective transport-reducing interventions are usually related to better provision of water (such as well construction) and energy-supply facilities and the provision of grinding mills near households. Most countries have policies of providing primary social services (for example, primary schools and dispensaries) at the village level, while secondary level units are provided at more central places. For social services, improving *quality* is often a more serious concern than improving *location*.[26]

Rural Transport Infrastructure (RTI): Complementing means of transport and the location and quality of facilities is the third element of rural transport—RTI. The main requirement for the sustainable delivery of RTI is a conducive framework for management and finance. The framework should include effective resource allocation and a logical system for setting priorities. This, in turn, requires sound advice on design and appraisal. Few developing countries, however, have managed to establish a favorable paradigm for managing and financing RTI. In the cases of these countries, the focus should first be on the development of such a framework in collaboration with all key stakeholders.

Developing a Rural Transport Policy and Strategy: To address the issues mentioned above, to ensure that rural transport is an effective facilitator of rural development, and to coordinate the activities of the various actors in the sub-sector, it is essential that rural transport policies and strategies are formulated and implemented. This process must address a broad range of issues, including physical, financial, economic, social, and environmental aspects of rural transport, and must relate to existing rural development and general transport policies and strategies.[27] Without such a comprehensive policy and strategy framework, the management and financing of RTI, especially maintenance, often fails. It is therefore highly recommended that countries formulate and enact an explicit rural transport strategy prior to undertaking an RTI investment program.

What is Rural Transport Infrastructure?

RTI is the rural road, track, and path network on which the rural population performs its transport activities, which includes walking, transport by non-motorized and motorized vehicles, and haulage and transport of people by animals. RTI includes the intra- and near-village transport network, as well as the infrastructure that provides access to higher levels of the road network. Following are the key features of RTI (see also Figure 2.3.).

Ownership: By definition, RTI is the local access infrastructure that is normally owned by local governments and communities. Local government roads (LGR) usually have formally defined ownership arrangements, i.e., they are designated. Community RTI is usually undesignated, or not part of the formally recognized transport network. In the absence of a respective legal framework, community RTI belongs to communities. Even designated roads are sometimes informally adopted by the local communities, who take responsibility for their maintenance. However, the capacity of communities to own and take care of RTI is limited usually to the intra- and near-village network and to short links to the main road network.[28]

Managing and Financing: Many different arrangements exist for managing and financing RTI.[29] LGR are often better managed by more central agencies on behalf of local governments,[30] or through joint-services arrangements (such as in Guatemala). Financial resources available for RTI include transfers from central government (from the Treasury, dedicated road funds, or through donor financing), which should be leveraged to generate local resources in cash or in kind. In most cases, financial resources are extremely scarce, particularly for maintenance.

Physical Features: LGR are sometimes at least partly engineered, which means they have an elevated, above-water-level riding surface, side drains and cross-drainage structures, including bridges. The majority of them are single-lane gravel or earth roads. They connect villages to the higher classified road network but are usually relatively short—less than 20 kilometers. Community RTI consists mainly of tracks, paths and footbridges, and sometimes (partly) engineered roads. They should normally not exceed five kilometers in length to ensure that the community has the capacity to maintain it.[31]

Traffic Characteristics: Transport activities on RTI are performed to a large extent on foot, sometimes by intermediate means of transport (IMT),[32] such as bicycles and animal drawn carts, and sometimes by using the services of motorized transport. Average daily motorized four-wheeled traffic on the majority of the RTI network is below 50 vehicles per day (VPD), while non-motorized traffic (NMT) can be a multiple of this number. Although the network of LGR, on average, constitutes about 70 percent of the designated network, it carries only a small portion of the total traffic (10 to 20 percent of total vehicle-kilometers).

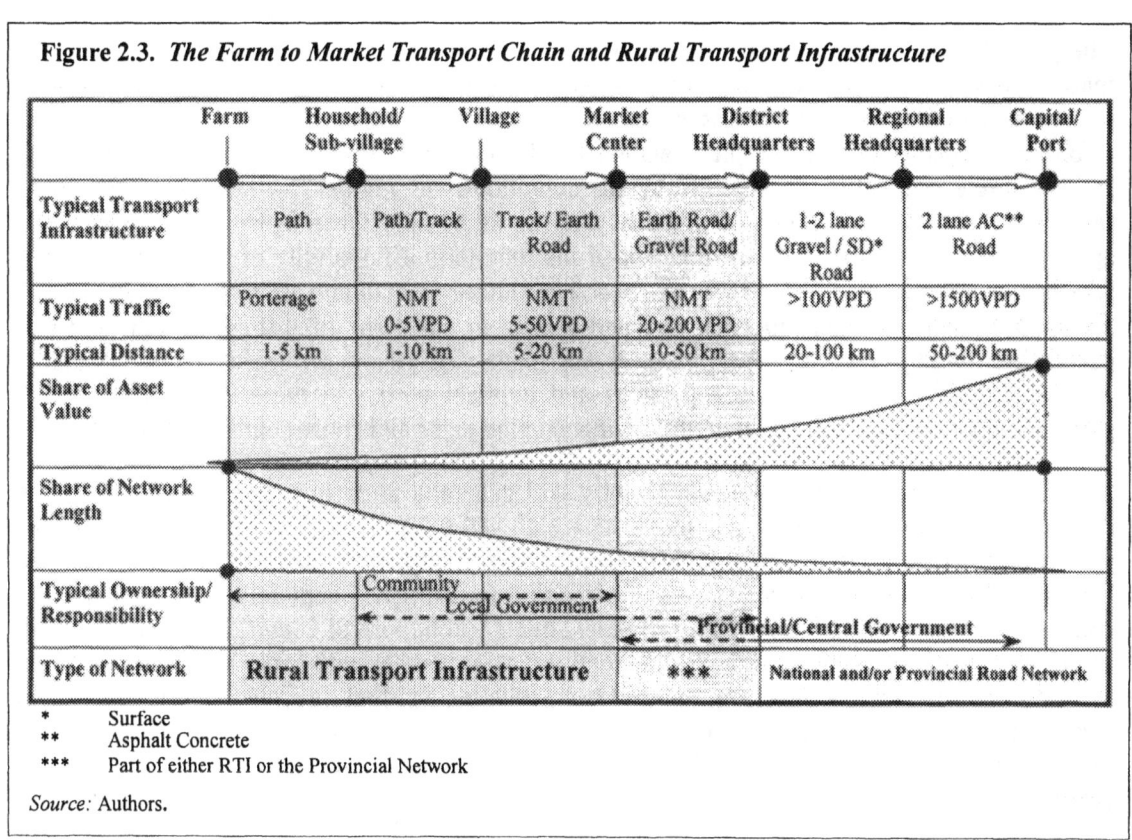

Figure 2.3. *The Farm to Market Transport Chain and Rural Transport Infrastructure*

* Surface
** Asphalt Concrete
*** Part of either RTI or the Provincial Network

Source: Authors.

A Basic Access Approach to RTI Investments

The RTI network is the lowest level of the physical transport chain that connects the rural population, and therefore the majority of the poor, to their farms, local markets, and social services, such as schools and health centers, potentially increasing their real income and improving their quality of life. A minimum level of service of the RTI network, referred to as *basic access*, is therefore one of the necessary building blocks of poverty reduction. In this context, the provision of basic access should be considered a basic human right, similar to the provision of basic health and basic education.[33]

In line with the poverty focus of RTI investments, a *basic access approach* is proposed which gives *priority to the provision of reliable, all-season access to as many villages as possible* over upgrading individual links to higher than necessary standards, thereby giving priority to network *equity*. The optimal distribution of available resources between such *equity*- and *growth*-oriented investments needs to be defined in each particular case. However, there is ample of evidence of "over-investment" on parts of the RTI and main road networks, and the potential for the transfer of resources to more equity-oriented investments is substantial.[34] A key indicator of network equity is the coverage of all-season access within one to two kilometers of rural households (see Appendix A).

A *basic access intervention* is defined as the least-cost intervention (in terms of total life-cycle cost) for providing reliable, all-season passability by the prevailing means of transport. If affordable (see next paragraph), this may mean all-season passability for a pick-up truck, a small bus, or a truck, even if these present only a small fraction of total traffic. However, it should be recognized that appropriate RTI is also required for the efficient and economical use of non-motorized (or intermediate) transport.[35]

The provision of motorable basic access roads is constrained by available resources, especially maintenance and capital budgets. What is affordable depends on the local population's capacity to maintain their own basic access infrastructure over the long-term.[36] Determining what is affordable depends on the complex relationship between this local capacity, available skills, income levels, population density, geographic conditions, and political will.[37] Appraising these factors will shed light on RTI sustainability, and should be undertaken as part of the investment appraisal process. Another broad indicator of the long-term affordability of RTI investments is whether or not a country has the capacity and resources to maintain its main road network.[38] Below a certain per capita income, and particularly in situations of difficult terrain and low population density, even least-cost basic access roads will not be affordable (notwithstanding existing suitable management arrangements and political will). In these cases, basic access provision may need to be focused on improving existing paths and constructing footbridges.

The road infrastructure of a particular country will generally grow in proportion to its level of development. Gradually, the originally existing path and track network will develop into a road network until finally all the households are served with road access, as is the case in developed countries.[39] To assist the understanding of network affordability, it is therefore recommended to compare road network indicators of a particular country with those of countries of a similar level of development. Appendix A provides the rural transport planner with some basic road network, mobility and accessibility data from selected low-, middle-, and high-income countries. The data demonstrate the relatively high burden of infrastructure cost and high existing inaccessibility in low-income countries. Moreover, the table shows that almost universally, motorized mobility grows proportionally to GDP.

3. DESIGNING RTI FOR BASIC ACCESS

This chapter discusses engineering design requirements for RTI. A differentiation is made between four categories of access: no, partial, full, and basic access, with a subsequent focus on the specific requirements of basic access. Design requirements for full access are ignored here, since they are substantially covered in the existing literature. As discussed in the previous chapter, basic access is defined as the level of service which provides the minimum accessibility required for rural socioeconomic development. In a majority of situations, where traffic is below 50 motorized four-wheeled vehicles per day (VPD), this means (trouble) spot improved, single-lane gravel or earth roads. If these are not affordable, the provision of basic access could involve the improvement of paths and construction of footbridges. Some guidelines for the engineering design of basic-access roads, paths, and low-cost structures for different climates and terrain are discussed in this chapter. More technical guidelines for the design of basic access roads are given in Appendix B, and those for paths and footbridges can be found in Appendix C.

Access and "Level of Service"

It can be useful to think of RTI, and its impact on "accessibility," from the perspective of "level of service." The following four levels of service, or access, need to be considered:

- **No (motorized) access:** defined as no motorized access within one to two kilometers of a household or a village;

- **Partial access:** defined as motorized access with interruptions during substantial periods of the year (the rainy season);

- **Full access:** defined as uninterrupted all-year, high quality (high-speed, low-roughness) access, and

- **Basic access:** defined as reliable all-season access for the prevailing means of transport, with limited periods of inaccessibility.

No Access or Partial Access: A substantial portion of the rural population in developing countries still does not have motorized access to transport networks at all, or only unreliable or partial access.[40] This portion of the population is nearly always less well-off compared to those who have reliable access.[41] Due to the low density of the unconnected population, the path and track network that connects them to the existing road network is vast, and is often several times its length.[42] To upgrade this network to even basic access standard, and maintain it at that level, would require enormous resources which in most cases are not available. Furthermore, in many situations the concerned population, if provided with motorable roads, could not afford motorized transport services, let alone private motor vehicles. Therefore, as the previous chapter has attempted to show, when resources are available to ease the transport burden of the unconnected populations, they should be carefully spent on a variety of access-enhancing measures, which may include basic access RTI.

Full Access: Full access means the provision of a fully engineered road with a consistent cross-section throughout its alignment and water crossings of high standard.[43] Such designs, which are considered the minimal standard for rural roads in many countries, are usually based on "design speed," and are to provide uninterrupted access throughout the year. Costs for a fully engineered rural road will typically be in the range of $20,000 to $100,000 per kilometer. Justification for such standards must be made on economic grounds (see Chapter 4), which is usually not possible on RTI with prevailing traffic levels of less than 50 VPD.[44] Literature on the design of fully engineered rural roads abounds, and this paper will not deal with the issue.[45]

Basic Access

The challenge in meeting basic access needs is deriving standards that can deliver the minimum level of service necessary to promote and sustain the development of rural communities, while providing such access to as many people as possible. Given the practical requirements of rural household socioeconomic activities, basic access RTI should meet the following minimum criteria:

- **Passability or reliability:** One of the most important aspects of basic access is passability or reliability. While it may be technically difficult to define when a road or a path becomes impassable, the impacts on the well-being and livelihood of the population from unreliable access are severe and well-documented.[46] The first priority for transport operators is the safety of their vehicles or animals, and they will often not travel if they consider a road or a path impassable—even if it is a decision based on unreliable information.

- **Adequate access to higher-level networks:** Functioning transport requires integrated systems. Access to main markets, to non-agricultural job opportunities, to higher-level health and educational facilities, and to administrative services requires reliable and affordable access from the community to the higher-level regional or national transport network.

- **Adequate access to local social and economic facilities:** Appropriate access to primary health and education facilities, and to local markets, both by the household and from the outside for the supply of inputs, is a fundamental requirement of basic access.

- **Adequate access to domestic activities:** Improved basic access infrastructure must reduce the time that households, particularly women and their daughters, spend on domestic activities, such as water and firewood collection, trips to the fields and to the grinding mill. It must enhance their productivity, and improve their lives and those of their families.

- **Trafficable by prevailing rural transport vehicle:** Basic access infrastructure must ensure that the prevailing type of rural transport vehicles (motorized or non-motorized) can expect reliable access. Reasonable levels of delays at river crossings or temporary road closings during the rainy season must be tolerated. Accepting such temporary closures can reduce investment costs considerably, as is shown later in this chapter. The maximum time allowed for temporary closures is both a political decision and an affordability issue.[47]

Basic Access "Standards" and Key Design Considerations: RTI standards, in countries where they exist, are often far in excess of what can be economically justified or what is necessary for the provision of basic access. The definition of the standards of basic access is ultimately a political matter and will depend on the development objectives, budget constraints, and social and natural environment of a particular country. In industrial countries, where basic access needs are nearly universally met, the standards of access roads are often defined on the basis of comfort and are not subjected to rigorous economic analysis.[48] On the other hand, in developing countries, where isolation and poverty are key targets of development investments, and resources are usually very limited, least-cost and economic criteria are required for maximizing the impact of interventions.

The removal of surface water is crucial for the success of basic access RTI, since at this traffic level, the weather causes more damage than does the traffic.[49] This means that a good camber of 5 to 8 percent, adequate side drains, and carefully designed cross drainage structures are required. Stone or concrete drifts, or splashes, are acceptable as a substitute for culverts. Major river crossings can be designed to allow traffic passage at low flows, and be closed at high flows. In many situations, peak flows may only last for a short duration (less than three hours). However, where rivers can not to be crossed for long periods, high-level and relatively expensive crossings should be provided to achieve basic access standards. If these are not affordable, providing an all-season footbridge should be considered, to allow pedestrian and IMT crossings during the rainy season.

Although roughness and speed are not important design parameters for basic access RTI, there are certain limits of roughness that should not be exceeded to avoid damage to vehicles. Speeds should normally not exceed 30 km/h, taking into account the varied use of basic access roads, by people, non-motorized, and motorized traffic on the carriage way. The most important criterion for the infrastructure is to be able to withstand the elements and traffic without extensive damage.

The (Trouble) Spot Improvement Approach: Many rural communities are still without road access. Connecting them will be a slow process. Increasingly, however, the situation faced by the rural transport planner is a deteriorating network of roads, tracks, and paths, passable only in the dry season, with difficulty, and not at all in the rainy season. In these situations, the spot improvement approach, focusing interventions only on difficult sections, is an appropriate method to provide basic access at a lower cost.

Spot improvement interventions require considerable judgment on the part of the design engineer. The types of interventions will vary according to the terrain, weather, and vehicle types. However, the construction cost savings can be in the order of 50 to 90 percent when compared to full improvement.

Road failure is most likely to occur on steep hills, at water crossings, and in low-lying areas. Solutions include realignment, paving of steep sections, provision of simple but permanent water crossings, and raising low-lying areas on embankments (see Appendix B). All interventions must be properly designed and engineered, but will only apply to a specific spot. In many situations, upgrading an existing track or earth road to basic access standard will only require interventions on 10 percent of the road length—greatly lowering the costs of providing all-season passability.

It is essential to ensure that untreated sections have sufficient capacity for the prevailing conditions and transport types. If the in-situ soils are incapable of bearing traffic loads when soaked, then it may be necessary to provide camber and drainage throughout. If the soils are not of sufficient strength, even in this condition, then a gravel surface should be provided throughout. During the design process, each section must be carefully analyzed in order to find the least-cost solution.

It is also essential to remember that very limited resources will be available for maintenance. Maintenance should not be confused with rehabilitation. If there is any concern that untreated sections will require more attention than basic vegetation clearing, cleaning drainage facilities, and minor surface reshaping to retain access, then a more substantial intervention should be undertaken. On the other hand, the spot improvement approach also applies to periodic maintenance, where in many situations spot regravelling, instead of full gravelling, is the right approach.

There is generally a great deal of resistance to spot improvement as a technical solution, especially in donor-financed interventions. A number of issues need to be addressed if this approach is to be pursued effectively:

- **Political pressure:** Politicians who are responsible for marshaling funds (including donor financing) for sector investments must answer to their constituencies, and therefore are under pressure to demonstrate effective and visible outcomes. This often leads to a decision to rehabilitate roads to fully engineered standards, rather than to undertake less visible spot improvements.

- **Road agency resistance:** Road engineers and managers want to remove particularly troublesome roads from their work programs. They may also view it as inappropriate to use "borrowed" donor money to produce what could be considered an inferior product. Many engineers are not well-informed about the merits of the spot improvement approach.

- **Private sector incentives:** Contractors and consultants prefer continuous upgrading to spot improvements. Upgrading (which entails higher quantities of earth movements and materials) is often the basis for mark-ups and therefore directly affects profits. Smaller, decentralized, and less visible spot improvements are viewed as unprofitable and are also difficult to define and supervise. Small-scale local contractors, however, may find this type of work very suitable.

- **Donor preferences:** Donor agencies often prefer a fully rehabilitated road to the process of identifying and financing investments in a series of dispersed trouble spots. Individual project financing may favor a quickly executed fully engineered approach because of the short time frame and the requirement to fully disburse funds. However, a long-term program approach is more appropriate for the gradual spot-improvement of a rural access network.[50]

In addition to the above-mentioned problems, spot improvement approaches will not work in areas that have very poor soils or are prone to flooding. Despite these problems, there is a strong case for the spot improvement approach. Without it, most developing countries simply cannot afford to provide basic access to the majority of their rural populations. An example of a successful spot improvement program is given in Box 3.1. Further good examples of successful spot improvement programs exist.[51]

Great potential for furthering the spot improvement approach is also seen in the implementation of performance-based road management and maintenance contracts. Until recently, these contracts have only been applied on major highways, and not on low-volume unpaved roads. A recent World Bank-financed project in Chad is proposing to introduce such types of contracts on approximately 450 kilometers of the unpaved main road network.[52] Performance criteria are: (a) passability at all times; and the assurance of (b) a specified average speed; (c) minimal riding comfort; and (d) road durability and preservation. This type of contract should guarantee an approach whereby the contractor, in his own self-interest, will focus on the critical spots of the network, while assuring a minimal comfort for the road user.

> **Box 3.1.** *The Roads 2000 Program in Kenya: A Spot Improvement and Labor-Based Approach to Network Rehabilitation and Maintenance*
>
> The Roads 2000 Program is a maintenance implementation strategy that supports a number of policy objectives of the Kenya Road Maintenance Initiative. It was developed as a solution to the deteriorating unpaved road network of 53,000 km. Road condition surveys identified a limited number of trouble spots, rather than general conditions, as the main cause of non-trafficable roads. Furthermore, the surveys found that the traditional equipment-based maintenance approach could not provide the required services with the current funding levels.
>
> Building on the successful experience of the labor-based Rural Access and Minor Roads Programs, Roads 2000 adopted a new approach to rapidly bring the network up to a maintainable standard and place it under effective maintenance with the optimum use of local resources.
>
> The three principal components of the Roads 2000 approach were:
>
> - Rehabilitation Phase: Bring roads back to minimum maintainable standard
> - Routine Maintenance: Establish labor-based maintenance system
> - Spot Improvement: Plan and carry out a follow-up program of selected spot improvements
>
> During initial preparation work, the road was brought to a passable and maintainable standard by labor units. The role of these work-units was to clear the vegetation and drainage system and re-establish the road camber.
>
> This preparation phase was followed by the establishment of small-scale contractors (group or single person contracts) to carry out routine maintenance on a permanent basis. On the more heavily-trafficked roads (> 50vpd), they were supported by tractor-towed graders.
>
> During the rehabilitation phase, required spot improvements were identified and implemented as funds and resources allowed. Typical works included:
>
> - Installation of new culverts (on average one new line per km);
> - Replacement or rehabilitation of existing culverts;
> - Spot regravelling (to a maximum of 4 percent of the road network length);
> - Provision of alternative surfacing over limited distance (for example, steep sections, approaches to structures);
> - Full road reconstruction over a limited distance; and
> - Bridge and drift rehabilitation;
>
> The following costs have been established for unpaved roads (adjusted to year 2000 prices):
>
> - Partial rehabilitation and spot improvement $ 2,000 / KM
> - Labor-only routine maintenance $240 / KM / Year
> - Routine towed grading $280 / KM
>
> *Source:* Authors.

Staged Construction—Not Recommended for RTI: [53] Staged construction is understood here as investment into structural elements of RTI to accommodate upgrading needs which might be required in the future due to traffic growth. This could mean, for example, the straightening of the vertical or horizontal alignment of an existing basic access road to accommodate a future fully engineered road, the provision of "two-lane" culverts for a single lane road, or the construction of two-lane bridges, where currently single-lane structures would be sufficient. While it might be possible to demonstrate long-term savings through staged construction in the case of trunk or provincial roads, where substantial traffic growth can be expected, the same is normally not possible for RTI, especially when initial traffic levels are very low. Where road agencies insist on such "advance" investments, economic analysis (see Chapter 4) should be carried out to determine their justification. Such analysis must take into account the additional short-term maintenance because of higher-than-necessary investments.

Engineering Design of Basic Access RTI

Basic access RTI has to be properly designed if it is to resist the weather and traffic, and produce a maintainable and sustainable asset. Unfortunately, even where the private sector is well developed, local consultants may have limited experience in the design of this type of rural project. It is necessary to produce designs, specifications, and quantities so they can be packaged out to small-scale contractors and supervised in a cost-effective manner. In addition, the designs themselves must be cost-effective, considering the low cost of the planned infrastructure (design costs should not exceed 6 percent of investment costs). There is limited experience in using local consultants for these services, and design tends to be carried out by technical assistance consultants recruited by projects and programs as part of a technical support package. For long-term sustainability, there is a need to stimulate the involvement of the local consulting industry. For assistance to communities, local NGOs are often the right partners and should be given the opportunity to acquire the necessary engineering skills.

With appropriate terms of reference that clearly specify the required approach, and specially designed training programs for local consulting firms, it is possible to secure local professional services. The absence of the time-consuming tasks involved in a fully surveyed design, detailed bill of quantities, and re-measurement serves to reduce costs. However, there is a much greater need for exercising engineering judgment in the design (and the supervision) of project work. The essential requirements for engineering services for basic access RTI are summarized in Appendix B.

Design Considerations—Traffic, Safety, Environment, and Social Impact: The engineering design needs to take into account a few key design considerations. These are related to the type of traffic use expected on the RTI, road safety considerations, the expected impact on the environment, and the social impact of RTI interventions. These requirements are explained in the paragraphs below.

Traffic: A wide variety of motorized and non-motorized traffic should be expected on RTI. However, roads and structures need to be designed to allow the largest and heaviest users to pass safely without damaging the structures. Often these largest users are seven-ton trucks, and, in other cases, pick-up trucks or motorcycles, and power tillers. In some cases, a design for non-motorized means of transport might suffice. Design to a low standard suitable only for 4WD-drive vehicles should normally be avoided, since these vehicles are rarely used by local transporters or the local population.

One potential problem is the possibility of large trucks using the road to evacuate heavy natural products and resources, such as crops, timber, minerals, etc. One excessively heavy truck can destroy the running surface of a basic access road. The likelihood of such traffic must be confirmed at project appraisal. Ideally, such traffic should be excluded by barriers (width and height restrictions at the start of the road), at the very least during the rainy season. If it is considered impossible to exclude such traffic, then the road must be designed for it, and systems put in place to ensure that the operators contribute their disproportionate share of maintenance costs.[54]

Because traffic levels will determine the type of intervention necessary (for example, basic versus full access), a thorough traffic survey is a prerequisite for all RTI interventions. In order to keep costs down to acceptable levels, it is necessary to select a few strategically correct locations (between villages). If resources are scarce, traffic counts can be correlated with population figures along different alignments in order to establish traffic estimates for links where traffic counts were not possible. Seven-day, 12-hour counts at selected locations are recommended to capture weekly variations. If possible, these can be complemented by counts during various times of the year to capture seasonal variations, as well as origin-destination and trip-purpose surveys. Both motorized and non-motorized traffic should be counted. Special consideration should be given to traffic-generating facilities such as hospitals, natural resource exploiting activities, or others. In Appendix D, low-cost traffic survey methodologies are presented.

Road Safety: Road safety is of primary importance for all road users. However, the safety concerns of basic access RTI are different than those for higher-level infrastructure. Typical problems are single-vehicle accidents and accidents between motorized and non-motorized vehicles, pedestrians and animals. Economic considerations will normally not allow separation of different modes of transport, and it must be accepted that foot and wheeled traffic of different speeds will intermingle in the traffic stream (exceptions see last paragraph of this sub-chapter).

The challenge for the rural transport planner is, therefore, to ensure that the speed of motorized traffic is low, say, not more than 30 km/h, particularly within villages. Spot improved, winding, single-lane roads with a relatively rough surface will, to an extent, automatically achieve this. However, it might be necessary to slow down traffic even more by narrowing the roads on straight sections (similar to urban traffic-calming designs). In such cases, it is essential for sight distances to remain in proportion to vehicle speeds.

On long, straight sections of flat terrain, the provision of trees adjacent to (but set back slightly from) the edge of the road (as is a common practice in Bangladesh) will have the effect of visually narrowing the road and slowing traffic, while providing shade and refuge to foot traffic. Where there is a sharp bend on such roads, painting middle sections of the tree trunks on the approaches to such bends can provide delineation and advance warning of the bend at night or in conditions of poor visibility.

All bridges, drifts, and culvert headwalls should be clearly marked with paint. Road widths must be consistent (even if consistently narrow, except for designated passing, vehicle loading or parking places), and weak road edges next to dangerous drops should be fenced (local bush fencing is acceptable, if maintained. However, metal road furniture such as signs and barriers often have limited life spans in resource-starved rural areas). The objective is to alert unfamiliar road users to obstacles and hazards ahead, so they can pass them safely.

It is often argued that since single-lane roads with passing places are inherently dangerous, wider roads should be built for safety reasons even when the traffic levels are low. However, the risk of vehicle-to-vehicle collision only increases slightly,[55] even if the volumes increase from 10 vehicles per day to 50 vehicles per day, and this level of traffic can be accommodated by passing places. However, where the road is expected to carry large volumes of pedestrian, or NMT, consideration needs to be given to their safety and a wider road shoulder or separate pedestrian and NMT-ways should be constructed (particularly within villages).

Environmental and Social Impact Mitigation: Basic access RTI interventions have both direct and indirect environmental and social impacts. Improved access might require the acquisition of productive agricultural land and housing, which might necessitate resettlement. Such resettlement will likely be minimal in the case of improvements to existing roads.[56] Other major direct environmental impacts are dust from vehicles and erosion of RTI surfaces, drainage structures, and outlets. Indirect impacts are the opening up of previously inaccessible, or marginally accessible, territory to immigration and resource harvesting.

The processes that help to identify and mitigate the potentially adverse impacts of RTI projects, while enhancing their positive effects, are the environmental assessment (EA) and social assessment (SA). Both EA and SA processes must be initiated at the beginning of the project cycle and continued throughout. To make them sustainable, they need to involve local experience and must be done with the participation of the local communities. Particularly in the case of new RTI, the SA might be extended to include studies encompassing baseline, mid-term and ex-post socioeconomic data collection, contrasting these with appropriately selected control areas to enable the monitoring and evaluation of the planned poverty-alleviating impact of the project. For this purpose, data will need to be collected at both the household and the community level from appropriate sample populations in the influence area.

The EA process involves six primary elements: a study of the baseline conditions in the region to establish benchmarks; an analysis of the existing institutional, legal, and administrative frameworks with respect to implementation; identification of potential environmental impacts; mitigation measures; an analysis of alternatives; and an environmental management action plan (EMAP). The EMAP is the output of the EA process and reflects the main impacts at major stages of the project, the relevant mitigation measures, the time-frame of their implementation, the institutional responsibilities, the costs, and the appropriate references to the contract documents.[57] The result of the SA might be a Resettlement Action Plan (RAP). Since the RAP is demand-driven, its implementation needs to be participatory and locally based. Involving experienced NGOs in the implementation is strongly recommended.

The need for EA and SA processes will vary greatly with the type of RTI intervention. In the case of small-scale improvement on existing networks, EA and SA might not be required at all, while in the case of new roads and particularly in mountainous areas, these processes might be extremely demanding. Relevant information on EA and SA can be found in the World Bank's Operational Manual and other relevant literature.[58]

Implementation Methods

Labor-Based Technology: The application of labor-based approaches to basic access RTI interventions contributes to their poverty-alleviating impact. Constructing RTI with labor-based methods requires between 2,000 and 12,000 person-days per kilometer for construction and 200 to 400 person-days per kilometer for maintenance. Utilizing local labor allows the local community to earn wages, as does procuring materials and tools from local sources. Furthermore, labor-based methods contribute to local empowerment through skills-transfer and creation of ownership. Also, if correctly designed, labor-based methods can have a substantial gender-specific impact.[59]

The type of work associated with basic access is ideal for labor-based methods. Spot improvement interventions are small-scale and varied, requiring attention to detail, and often do not require heavy construction equipment. In the case of community RTI, the full involvement of the community gives them the opportunity to acquire the skills for the eventual infrastructure maintenance by labor-based methods. It is important to note that equipment (for example, graders) are seldom available for subsequent maintenance activity for RTI, a fact that should be planned for at design.

There are certain prerequisites for effective labor-based contract execution, including labor availability in sufficient numbers, supervision experience, and the availability of qualified contractors. These contractors must be small-scale and have experience in labor-based project execution. They should possess, or have access to the appropriate equipment. If they have no direct experience in labor-based execution of works, they must at least be willing to undergo respective training.[60] Box 3.2 elaborates on the relevance of labor-based approaches.

> **Box 3.2.** *Relevance of Labor-Based Execution*
>
> Road construction and maintenance works are often described as equipment-based or labor-based, depending on the relative intensity of productive factor use. The term "labor-based" is used to describe projects where labor is substituted for equipment when it is cost-effective. This covers most road-related activities apart from compaction and heavy earthworks. The term also includes the use of appropriate light equipment (mostly tractor-trailer) which supports the utilization of labor in specific essential activities such as compaction and gravel haulage for surfacing.
>
> In most developing countries, especially in rural areas, unemployment is high, jobs are scarce, and the average daily wage rate for workers in the agricultural sector is somewhere between less than $1 and $5 per day. Equipment is usually owned by a few large-scale contractors or government departments. Maintenance and back-up services can be problematic and expensive, and real equipment costs are prohibitively high. The lower unit-cost of labor relative to capital therefore makes labor-based road works both economical and socially desirable.
>
> In their recent publication *Employment-Intensive Infrastructure Programs: Labor Policies and Practices, 1998*, the International Labor Organization concludes that* labor-based construction and maintenance: (a) was about 10 percent to 30 percent less costly, in financial terms, than more equipment-intensive works; (b) reduced foreign exchange requirements by 50 percent to 60 percent; and (c) created, for the same amount of investment, two to five times more employment.
>
> Several important factors contribute to the viability of labor-based construction techniques, such as government attitude, economic conditions (especially labor and capital markets), the location of the project, road agency administrative and financial procedures, capacity for management and human resource development, and the provision of adequate training.
>
> * Based on comparative studies carried out in a number of countries, such as Ghana, Lesotho, Madagascar, Rwanda, Zimbabwe, Cambodia, Lao People's Democratic Republic (Lao PDR) and Thailand.
>
> *Source:* Authors.

Despite these advantages, it has been difficult to mainstream labor-based approaches. The difficulties encountered include inflexible labor laws, the availability of cheap second-hand heavy equipment, unsuitable procurement laws, and a lack of capacity to rapidly pay labor-based contractors.[61] To mainstream labor-based approaches, these obstacles need to be overcome at the policy level.

Small-Scale Contractor Development: By their very nature, basic access interventions are small-scale, varied, and scattered. The work is ideal for execution by small-scale labor-based contractors and by community contracts. Such types of contracting require (a) an appropriate policy environment; (b) capacity building programs for designing, managing, and execution of contracts; and (c) appropriate procurement procedures.

Considerable experience is available for the development of small-scale labor-based contractors.[62] An enabling environment must be created. If the contractors are to survive, they require a regular workload, rapid payment of bills, and access to credit facilities and equipment rental opportunities. The key is the management capacity of the contracting agency. To overcome capacity constraints at the local government level, it is often recommended that government entities join together to form joint-services committees or hire consultants to assist in contract management.[63] Contractors' associations have an important role to play in the capacity building process as well.[64]

The limited capacity of single small-scale contractors may require the employment of numerous contractors if major earthworks are involved (average capacity will be about 1 km of earthworks per month and 0.5 km of gravelling per month). Part of the capacity building process is assistance to the contractors with appropriate equipment, which in most cases is tractor-towed equipment, such as trailers, water bowsers, rollers and towed graders.[65]

Community Contracting: Community contracting has become a major means of channeling grant funding to the rural poor. Community contracting means procurement by, on behalf of, or from communities. Implementing agencies are the communities themselves who take direct responsibility for their own development, and the role of government here is to provide facilitating support (usually through the assistance of NGOs). Participation from the community has to be an overriding consideration in designing the various procedures, including procurement and disbursement. Simplified procurement procedures for community contracting are required.[66] Experience from such community-based investment operations has shown that participation greatly assists accountability. A key feature for successful community contracting is the existence of a legal framework that gives communities legal status, without which they are unable to receive or manage funds.

Maintenance of Basic Access RTI

A common feature of RTI is insufficient or non-existent maintenance. Financial allocations to RTI maintenance are almost always inadequate, both relative to the main road network and compared to general expenditures for construction.[67] Moreover, capacity to execute maintenance is lacking. A good indicator for the lack of maintenance capacity is the need for rehabilitation, which by definition is caused by a lack of maintenance. Earth and gravel roads and paths are very vulnerable to the elements and will often not survive a single season without proper maintenance. A road or path is no better than its weakest link, and one failed drainage structure or section can be sufficient to disrupt access. The principle roots of maintenance neglect are institutional and financial. These must be addressed prior to any consideration of investments in RTI.[68]

Maintaining an earth or gravel road is relatively costly. As a rule of thumb, undiscounted maintenance costs over the typical life of RTI will equal the initial construction costs. For example, a typical $5,000/km basic access road may cost an average of $250 a year per km to maintain over its assumed twenty-year life.

From an engineering point of view, there are important tradeoffs between routine, recurrent, and periodic maintenance, and further investments. Often, enhanced routine maintenance is able to provide the required "passability," which reduces the need for periodic maintenance or further investments in the form of spot improvements. This is of particular importance with respect to periodic maintenance.[69] In many developing countries, reserves of naturally occurring gravel used for periodic renewal of gravel layers are simply no longer available. The maintenance of a proper camber and the protection of drainage structures will reduce the need for periodic maintenance and rehabilitation. If comparing the costs of increasing the grading frequency on earth roads against gravelling at low traffic levels, the former is usually much more economical.[70]

4. APPRAISING RTI FOR BASIC ACCESS

Appraisal, in the widest sense, includes the analysis and assessment of social, economic, financial, institutional, technical, and environmental issues related to a planned intervention. This chapter discusses appraisal in the context of participatory approaches for the selection and priority setting of RTI interventions and projects, as well as the economic rationale of the planning process. It also describes alternative screening and ranking methods, in particular cost-effectiveness and cost-benefit approaches. For further information on these methodologies, the reader is referred to the relevant literature.[71] For a discussion of technical issues, see the previous chapter. Examples of recent economic appraisals of World Bank financed RTI projects are given in Appendix E.

A Participatory Planning Approach

Local communities are the main stakeholders and users of RTI. In recognition of this, there is now wide acceptance that their participation in the preparation and implementation of investment programs enhances local ownership and commitment, and fosters better accountability, management and sustainability.[72]

Although ongoing decentralization efforts in many developing countries have made local governments and communities responsible for the provision of local facilities, including RTI, a comprehensive planning process for these assets has not usually been put in place. In a first step, at both the local government and community level, priorities must be assessed across sectors. Once the need for a RTI intervention or project has been agreed upon, care must be taken that maintenance of existing RTI is incorporated into the early stages of the planning process.

The planning framework must be built on a participatory and iterative process, simultaneously bottom-up and top-down. A national or state-based agency for RTI should set guidelines. However, the driving force of the process must consist of priority setting and consultations at the local government and community level.[73] For ensuring and building capacity for effective participation, in most cases it is necessary to employ local NGOs or consultants that are professionally trained in participatory methods.[74]

Local consultations are also emphasized in the planning process in industrialized countries that rarely apply strict economic analysis to capital investments for local roads. In developing countries, however, where resources are extremely scarce (and often provided by donors) coherent selection tools that include economic considerations and are understandable to the local planners and communities can usefully support the participatory decision-making process (for example by illustrating opportunity cost and incremental trade-offs).

It has been argued that participatory decision-making can replace the economic selection process. This might be the case if investments are entirely locally financed, but even then the "wish list" will typically be more sizeable than available resources and a rational process (using economic criteria) should be used to help prioritize alternative investments. However, even modest contributions from outside sources can make economic planning tools useful, since the outside funding agencies, be it a road fund, government or a donor agency, will need to be convinced that the proposed investment is a sound and prudent use of its contribution.

Local Transport Plans—A Key Tool for the Participatory Process: Key tools for the participatory planning process are local transport plans, in the form of elaborate local government (district) transport "master plans" or simple community transport sketches (Figure 4.1).

Comprehensive coverage of transport infrastructure (including roads, paths, waterways, etc.) and transport producing facilities (villages, schools, health centers markets, etc.) should be contained in these plans. Guidelines for their preparation should be provided by the focal institutional entity responsible for rural roads in the country.[75] The objectives and core design criteria for these plans should ideally be contained in a country's National Rural Transport Policy and Strategy. Furthermore, they should be based on regional development plans which reflect the various sector strategies (such as health, education, infrastructure and agricultural development). They should be prepared in a participatory way in close consultation with the communities. A complementary planning tool for the community level planning process is the Rural Accessibility Planning (RAP) (Box 4.1).

Box 4.1. *Rural Accessibility Planning (AP)*

To improve rural access effectively, an appropriate planning tool has been developed, with ILO technical assistance, through pilot projects in Asia and Africa. It partners with communities and local organizations to identify their access problems and propose solutions. AP focuses on the household, and measures its access needs in terms of time spent to get access. The underlying principle of AP is to reduce time spent on access which could then be spent on other activities.

Steps 1 and 2: Data Collection and Processing. Trained local enumerators collect data on household time spent and mode used to gain access to services and facilities. Processed data results in a demand-oriented access spread sheet for the target area.

Step 3: Preparation of Accessibility Profiles, Indicators and Maps. Access profiles for target areas cover basic information on location of facilities and services and the difficulties people have accessing them. Accessibly Indicators (AI) are calculated by multiplying the number of households (N) with the subtraction of the average travel time to a facility (T) minus the acceptable/target travel time Tm, times the frequency of travel (F): $AI = N*(T-Tm)*F$. Finally, maps are established with the available information.

Step 4: Prioritization. The larger the value of the AI, the greater the problem.

Steps 5, 6 and 7: Data Validation and Defining Targets and Objectives, and Project Identification. Results of the AP are presented and discussed in a participatory decision making workshop where pending on available budgets interventions are identified, which most effectively reduce time and efforts spent in obtaining access (including improved transport infrastructure, provision of means of transport and relocation of facilities).

Step 8: Implementation, Monitoring and Evaluation. Identified projects are integrated into the overall local planning system for implementation, monitoring and evaluation with local communities fully involved.

Source: Adapted from Fatemeh Ali-Nejadfard, 2000.

Most of the necessary data for the master plan can be obtained by means of a low-cost road and path inventory and condition survey conducted by local engineers or consultants in consultation with communities.[76] Planners and engineers conducting the survey assess the expenditure and type of works necessary to bring each link to basic access standard.[77] In addition, when existing traffic levels merit, the condition survey should assess the costs of bringing links to fully engineered standard. During the condition survey, traffic data (see Appendix D) and other information such as location of villages, schools, health centers and major traffic-generating facilities such as markets are collected simultaneously. On the basis of the condition survey and socioeconomic data, an "as is" map is established. An example is shown in Figure 4.1.

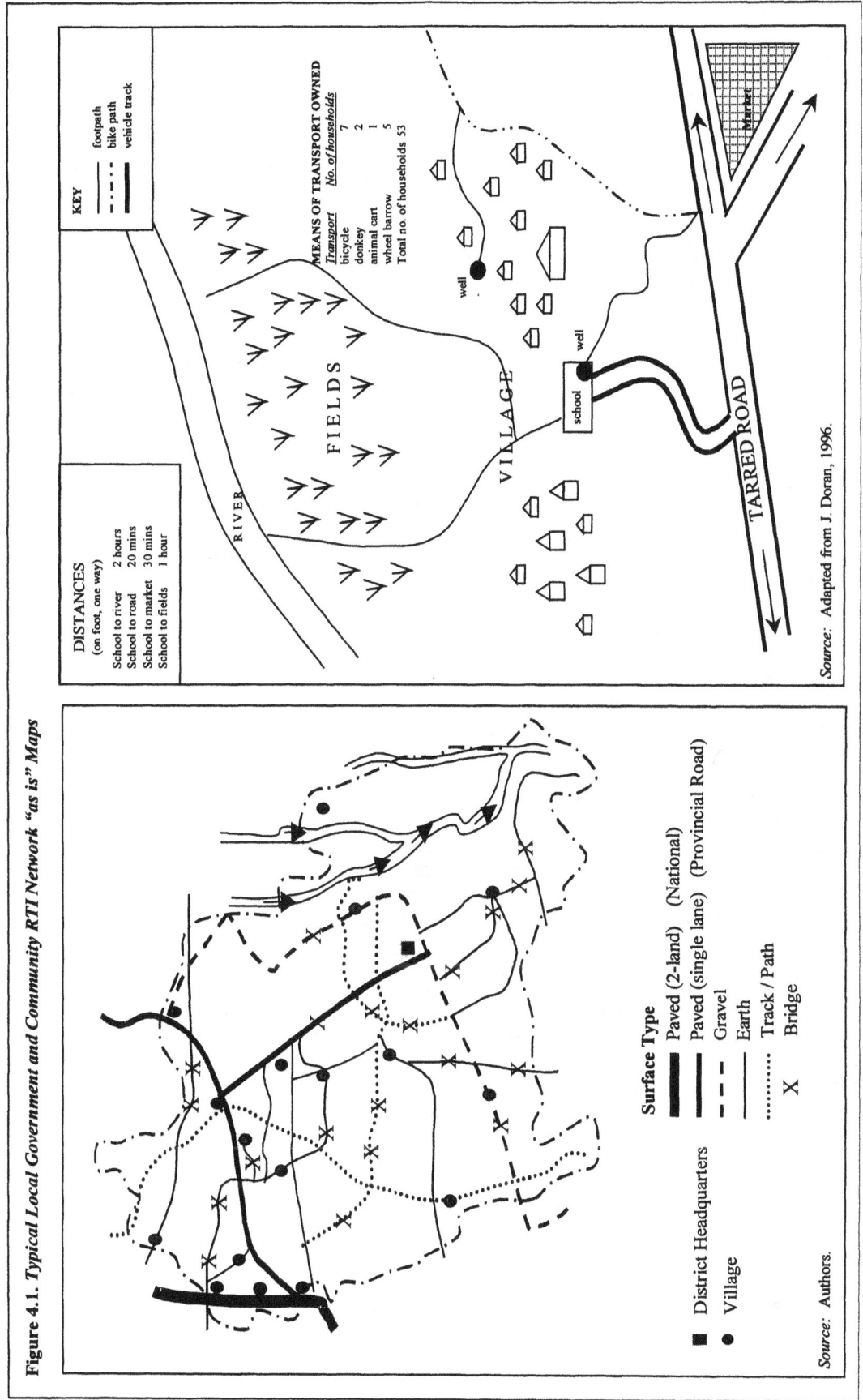

Figure 4.1. Typical Local Government and Community RTI Network "as is" Maps

Selection and Priority Setting Methods

Screening and Ranking: Selection and priority-setting methods for basic access RTI interventions consist of two broad types of methodologies which are usually applied in succession: (a) screening and (b) ranking. ***Screening*** decreases the number of investment alternatives given budgetary constraints, which may involve: (a) targeting disadvantaged areas or communities based on poverty indexes, or (b) eliminating investments into low-priority sections of the network selected based on agreed criteria.

Targeting Poor and Disadvantaged Communities: One of the purposes of screening is to target investments to disadvantaged regions, local governments and communities. Screening approaches were developed initially for targeting isolated or economically deprived communities and regions. They have since been adapted for the selection of districts, communities, and municipalities on the basis of poverty criteria—measuring economic standing and potential, as well as social development (such as literacy and health statistics). This might also be a useful approach for identifying areas adversely affected by structural adjustment measures or natural disaster. In China, for example, poverty-based pre-screening was used to identify "priority counties," with a second- and third-stage screening process was then used to identify specific road sections and corresponding design standards (Box 4.2).

Box 4.2. *Selecting Road Improvement Components for Poverty Alleviation*

Two recent Bank-financed highway projects in China (Second Henan Provincial Highway Project, 1996, and Second Shaanxi Provincial Highway Project, 1996) included a poverty-focused component. The component was proposed in line with the provincial government programs of Road Improvement for Poverty Alleviation (RIPA), which aimed to provide all-weather access through rehabilitation, upgrading, and construction of rural roads to a main provincial road axis for every poor county township and the majority of villages.

A three-stage screening procedure was developed to select rural roads to be included in the project's RIPA component. The first stage of screening identified the "priority counties" that were most in need of improved road transport as an element in alleviating their poverty. The criteria used to prioritize included average income per capita, number of the "very poor" per 10,000 population, value of agriculture production, value of mineral production, and other social development indicators (including literacy rate, health workers per thousand population, and access to clean drinking water).

The second stage of screening used a cost-effectiveness criterion to select rural road systems from these priority counties. In this stage, rural roads for improvement in these counties were grouped into the RIPA systems based on three criteria: (1) continuity of the system; (2) maximization of the population served; and (3) connectivity to as many settlements as possible. Then a cost-effectiveness criterion—the proposed investment cost divided by population served in the influence area of the system—was used to screen the RIPA road systems. The very high unit cost systems were dropped. Finally, available financial resources were taken into consideration in deciding the number of systems and size of the RIPA packages that passed this stage of the screening.

The third stage of screening consisted of an analysis of the economic and social benefits of each of the road systems included for consideration at the end of the second stage. The analysis also included a review of motorization trends to guide the selection of proper road class and road engineering design that would meet the future needs of both motorized and non-motorized traffic in these rural areas.

Source: Hajj and Pendakur, 2000.

Eliminating Low-Priority Links of the Network: Another use of screening is to eliminate low priority links from consideration for investments. For example, in the case of the district transport master planning process in Andhra Pradesh, it was decided that for each village only one link, normally the shortest one, would be upgraded to basic access standard. This reduced the road network that was considered for interventions from about 5000 kilometers to 3000 km per district (Figure 4.2 and Appendix E.1). There are many other examples of elimination by screening.[78]

Ranking: After screening methods have been applied to a given set of investment choices, resources are still unlikely to be sufficient to finance the balance of the remaining desirable interventions, and hence a ranking or prioritization exercise is required. The following three main ranking methods for RTI are discussed in the following paragraphs: (a) multi-criteria analysis; (b) cost-effectiveness analysis; and (c) cost-benefit analysis.

Multi-Criteria Analysis

Multi-criteria analysis (MCA) is commonly used to rank RTI investments. Criteria such as traffic level, proximity to health and educational facilities and agricultural assets receive weights (points) relative to their perceived importance. Each road link is then allocated the number of points corresponding to the fulfillment of the particular criteria. The aggregate number of points that each intervention receives is computed by simply adding the points allocated per indicator, or through the application of a more complex formula. The result of this process leads to a ranking of the investment options.

In most examples, indicators used under MCA implicitly reflect economic and subjective evaluations. If the weights and points are decided upon and allocated in a participatory way, MCA has the potential to be a participatory planning method based on implicit socioeconomic valuation. However, it tends to be applied by consultants or planners in isolation without consultation with the concerned users and stakeholders. The outcome of the MCA methodology, is often, unfortunately, non-transparent, especially if too many factors are considered and a complicated formula applied. Therefore, if adopted, this method has to be used with great care and kept simple, transparent, and participatory.

Cost-Effectiveness Analysis

A subset of the MCA is the cost-effectiveness analysis (CEA). CEA compares the cost of interventions with their intended impacts. CEA is widely used to appraise investments in the social sector, however, has rarely been used in the transport sector. This has largely been due to the belief that the impacts of transport interventions are mainly economic in nature and should be measured. With the increased focus on the poverty and social impacts of transport investments, and their justification on these broader grounds, CEA has recently become more prominent.

The operational policies[79] of the World Bank allow the use of CEA in situations where benefits cannot be measured in monetary terms, or where measurement is difficult. There are provisions, however, that (a) the objectives of the intervention are clearly stated and are part of a wider program of objectives (such as poverty alleviation); and (b) the intervention represents the least-cost way of attaining the stated objectives. "Least-cost" in the context of RTI means that "basic access standards" have been applied as elaborated in Chapter 3.

For example, one of the first Bank-financed rural transport projects where CEA was intensively used for the ranking of rural road investments was the Rural Roads Component of the Andhra Pradesh Economic Restructuring Project. The selection process used in this project is described in Figure 4.2. For a description of the economic analysis carried out, see Appendix E.1. The CEA was applied to rank individual links of a "core network" selected on the basis of screening criteria. The cost-effectiveness indicator was defined as the cost of improving a particular link to "basic access standard"[80] divided by the number of people served by the link.

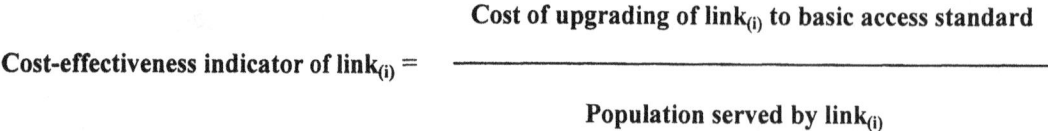

$$\text{Cost-effectiveness indicator of link}_{(i)} = \frac{\text{Cost of upgrading of link}_{(i)} \text{ to basic access standard}}{\text{Population served by link}_{(i)}}$$

On this basis, up to 700 individual links were ranked. In view of the available financing, it was then decided that the maximum amount of investment allowed per link would be $50 per person served.[81]

CEA also lends itself to the incorporation of poverty and other factors as is shown in Box 4.3 (for details on the economic analysis of this project see Appendix E.2).

Figure 4.2. *Applying the Basic Access Approach: Rural Road Component of the Andhra Pradesh Economic Restructuring Project*

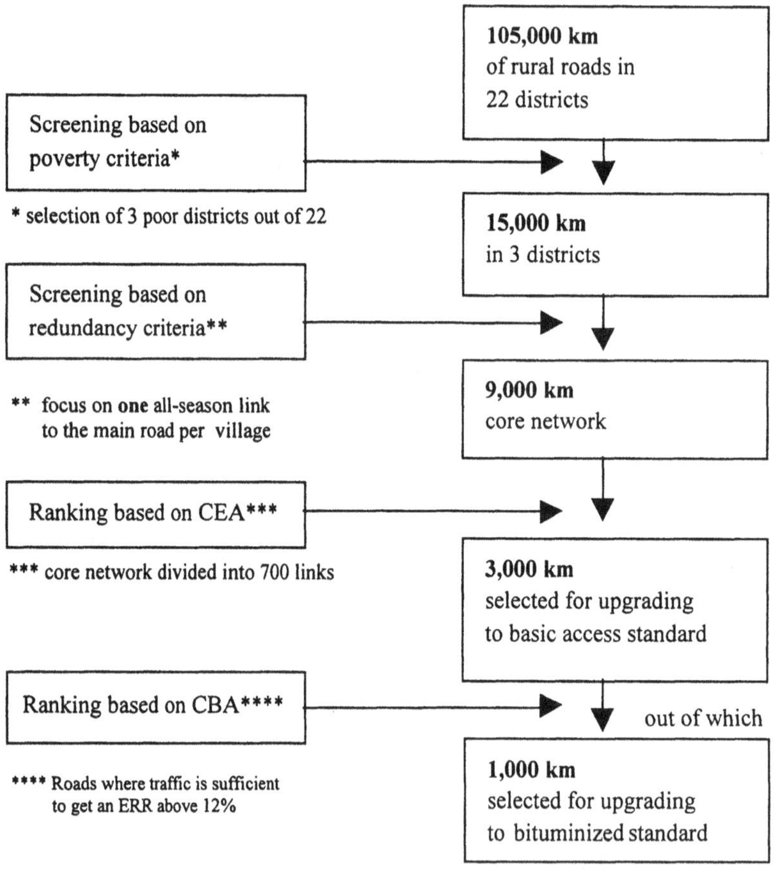

- Screening based on poverty criteria* → 105,000 km of rural roads in 22 districts
  - * selection of 3 poor districts out of 22
- Screening based on redundancy criteria** → 15,000 km in 3 districts
  - ** focus on **one** all-season link to the main road per village
- Ranking based on CEA*** → 9,000 km core network
  - *** core network divided into 700 links
- Ranking based on CBA**** → 3,000 km selected for upgrading to basic access standard
  - **** Roads where traffic is sufficient to get an ERR above 12%
- out of which → 1,000 km selected for upgrading to bituminized standard

Source: Authors.

Box 4.3. *Applying the Basic Access Approach: Vietnam's Second Rural Transport Project*

The overall goal of this project is to contribute to poverty reduction in rural Vietnam. To meet this objective, the project aims to provide "basic road access" to all communes in participating provinces. For purposes of the project, basic road access is defined as year-round motorized access from the commune center to the closest district center. District centers have many of the higher level facilities —hospitals, upper secondary schools, market centers. Effective year-round road access to the district center can be expected to make significant impacts on living standards in the communes.

A) Basic access roads: Before project implementation, it was not clear whether the budget would be sufficient to provide basic access roads to all communes; (there was also the possibility that it would be too much). A cost-effectiveness methodology that takes poverty, population and project costs into account was thus used to prioritize between eligible roads. Among the different groups in the population, the formula put about three times more weight on the poor than on the non-poor. The choice of three as the relative weight on the poor was discussed and agreed to in focus-group meetings with local non-transport experts and with the Ministry of Transport. The index for ranking alternative basic access roads is then:

$$CE_1 = (\text{\# of poor} + 0.3* \text{\# of non-poor})/\text{total cost of rehabilitation}$$

B) Selected rehabilitation and spot improvement on other roads: Once basic road access needs are met, remaining funding can be devoted to selected rehabilitation and upgrading of other roads. This budget is allocated to the highest priority road projects as determined by cost-effectiveness rankings based on a formula that takes into account poverty, population served, potential for agricultural development (as measured by unused land with agricultural potential and number of social and other facilities) and costs of the proposed works. The index for ranking roads for rehabilitation/spot improvement is:

$$CE_2 = \{[1 + (\text{unused land/per person}) + (\text{facilities /per person})]*[\text{\# of poor} + 0.3* \text{\# of non-poor}]\}/ \text{ total cost of rehabilitation}$$

Again, the choice of variables (subject to data availability) were discussed and agreed to in focus group meetings with local non-transport experts and with the ministry of transport.

Source: Dominique Van de Walle, 1999.

Thresholds for Cost-Effectiveness: Unlike CBA, where projects normally are deemed "uneconomic" when their ERR falls below 10-12%, there are no well established criteria for determining "opportunity cost" thresholds when ranking on the basis of cost-effectiveness. Such a determination is then left to policy makers. For example, if access can be provided to two, otherwise similar communities at $100 per person served and $50 per person served, respectively, cost-effectiveness criteria would clearly "rank" the latter community higher. However, the question that remains is whether $50 per capita is a sufficient "return" to justify intervention (could that $50 per person be spent with more impact in another sector, or would it yield an ERR of 10-12% considering the opportunity cost of capital in the country?). In practice, for basic access RTI, such thresholds do not usually become a point of debate, because project budgets are normally pre-set and are exhausted before what most planners agree are reasonable cost-effectiveness limits.

Sample Study to Indicate Economic Viability: To overcome the problem of open-ended thresholds associated with the CEA method, it may be desirable to complement the CEA method with a sample study based on cost-benefit analysis for one or two roads in the project area (see below). If this sample study can establish that a per-capita threshold of investment meets the prescribed economic rate of return for the sample link (such as the $50 used in the Andhra Pradesh appraisal mentioned above), then all links above the threshold are likely to be viable. Such an approach has been shown to provide a good economic basis for applying the CEA method to a broad RTI investment program, especially where socioeconomic characteristics do not vary greatly.

Cost-Benefit Analysis

A more common alternative to CEA is to undertake an economic evaluation of road investments using cost-benefit analysis (CBA). CBA is a comprehensive accounting of all the real costs and benefits associated with a project. In the case of road projects, this includes users and non-users, as well as road agency costs. Where the impact on non-users is negligible, a CBA of road alternatives centers around the trade-offs between total life-cycle costs of infrastructure (capital and maintenance) and user costs and benefits (operating cost of the primarily vehicle and time savings). The outcome of CBA permits ranking of alternative interventions on a particular link based on the net present value (NPV). Where a number of different but independent links are being considered (and there is a fixed capital budget) ranking can be based on the net present value per financial investment outlay ratio (NPV/INV), or net present value per kilometer (NPV/KM) if road infrastructure costs (capital and maintenance) are the same for all links. The benefit from cost savings for transport users can be considered an increase in "consumer surplus", if such savings accrue to the users as reduction in transport costs or charges. Alternatively, if transport cost reductions lower producers' input and output costs, and result in higher net income, then the benefits can be considered as an increase in "producers' surplus."[82]

Producer Surplus Methods are discussed in detail in the well known works of Carnemark, Beenhakker and others.[83] The method requires assumptions concerning the impact of transport investments on local agricultural productivity and output which are difficult to assess, particularly in a situation where interventions are expected to open up new areas and adequate production data may be difficult to compile. To the extent that RTI investments are increasingly focused on existing networks and often put more emphasis on social rather than economic objectives, the application and relevance of the producer surplus method has decreased in recent years.

Consumer Surplus Methods are well established and applied in road investment models, such as the Highway Development and Management Model, Version 4 (HDM-IV). The methods are reliable to apply to higher-volume roads (>200 VPD). However, its application to low-volume roads encounter problems related to the small magnitude of user benefits and the stronger influence of the environment rather than traffic on infrastructure deterioration. With traffic levels between 50 and 200 VPD, and particularly with regard to unpaved roads, a modified and customized approach can be taken, as is done in the recently developed Roads Economic Decision Model (RED) (see Appendix F). This method attempts to take into account uncertainty related to the input assumptions and an expanded treatment of user benefits (Box 4.4).

For traffic levels below 50 VPD, as is the case on the majority of RTI, the consumer surplus approach is usually not recommended because the main benefits from such projects are not from savings in motor vehicle operating costs, but relate to the provision of access itself. As discussed previously, for various reasons the benefits of access are difficult to quantify. Also, traffic on such very low volume RTI typically consists of a majority of non-motorized vehicles (where part of the costs are human energy needed to pull or push the vehicles, which cannot be easily priced), animal transport such as haulage by mules, walking and head loading (porterage). Therefore, the following section proposes some extensions or special adaptations to the traditional CBA and discusses their appropriate application for RTI.

> **Box 4.4.** *Roads Economic Decision Model (RED)*
>
> The Roads Economic Decision Model (RED) provides an approach for improving the decision-making process for the development and maintenance of low-volume roads. RED is a consumer surplus model designed to help evaluate investments in roads with traffic volumes between 50 and 200 vehicles per day. The model is implemented in a series of Excel workbooks that estimate vehicle operating costs and speeds, perform economic comparisons of investment and maintenance options, switching values and stochastic risk analysis.
>
> RED simplifies the economic evaluation process but at the same time addresses the following concerns related to low-volume roads: (a) reduces the input requirements; (b) takes into account the higher uncertainty related to the inputs; (c) computes internally generated traffic based on a defined price elasticity of demand to which induced traffic can also be added; (d) quantifies the economic costs associated with the days-per-year when the passage of vehicles is further disrupted by a highly deteriorated road condition; (e) optionally, uses vehicle speeds as a surrogate parameter to road roughness to define the level of service of low-volume roads; (f) includes road safety benefits; (g) includes in the analysis other benefits (or costs) such as those related to non-motorized traffic, social service delivery, and environmental impacts, if they are computed separately; and (h) presents the results with the capacity for sensitivity, switching values and stochastic risk analyses. RED can be downloaded free of charge at http://www.worldbank.org/html/fpd/transport/roads/tools.htm
>
> *Source:* Archondo-Callao, 1999.

Extending the CBA Framework for RTI

Because traditional CBA approaches do not account for many of the benefits of RTI investments, extending the framework of CBA holds promise for improved analysis. The proposed enhancements of traditional CBA techniques are aimed at finding broader measures of economic benefits and costs applicable to RTI. That is, while the principles of analysis are the same, the special features of RTI call for special methods of analysis. The methods described here can serve as a useful foundation for "pilot" or "sample" CBA to supplement CEA, or in the case of a low-volume road that presents a major investment, a new access option to a given area, or a proposed upgrading to a higher than basic access level. Possible enhancements of CBA include:

- Better assessment of the costs of interrupted access

- Estimating operating cost savings of NMT

- Savings due to mode changes (from NMT to motorized transport)

- Improved valuation of time savings, and

- Valuation of social benefits from improved access to schools and health centers

Better Assessment of the Cost of Interrupted Access: For cases where passability suffers during the rainy season, an assessment can be made of the extent of interruption. Seasonal changes in transport quality can be assessed on the basis of local socioeconomic impact, such as higher goods prices, lost productivity, or decreased social travel. In such cases, an assessment of the impact on particular activities may be necessary, since losses associated with seasonal interruptions will vary by activity (agriculture, marketing, travel for jobs and related wage earnings, school attendance and consequent decline in quality of education, health visits, etc). It may be difficult to directly observe the impact of seasonal access variations, and such information will usually need to be collected either through a local survey or other participatory processes. In addition, it may be possible to examine the costs associated with alternative (but longer) routes (that increase transport cost and time), or substitutes for transport (migration, storage), or even lost opportunities and income, to better understand the impact.

Estimating Operating Costs Savings of NMT: Methods for calculating the non-motorized transport user cost savings from road improvements have only recently become a part of project evaluation. Studies in Bangladesh and Indonesia have estimated user costs for a set of NMT and the results of these studies has been integrated in the HDM-4 model.[84] In particular circumstances, additional country- or area-specific field work may be necessary to get realistic estimates of NMT costs. Particular information is required regarding operating costs in relation to differing road surface conditions. Box 4.5 gives an example from Bangladesh.

Box 4.5. *Rickshaw Operating Costs in Bangladesh*

Studies in Bangladesh indicate how to realistically assess (changes in) the cost of transport services by rickshaws and rickshaw-vans that are used as a major form of rural transport The rickshaw-van is the most common NMT used for goods in rural Bangladesh, and it is driven (pedaled) by a van driver. It can carry about 400 kg weight per trip. Since the main cost of its operation is the time and food-energy used by its driver, its operating cost is difficult to estimate. For project analysis, therefore, charges actually made by the rickshaw-van operators on different types of road conditions were collected through surveys. The vehicle operating cost savings used in the study are based on actual differentials in charges between existing poor roads and improved roads, as they substantially reflect the cost variations due to greater exertion, time and additional food for higher level of effort and energy needed for plying on rougher roads. Since NMT transporters operate in a highly competitive market where there are no significant externalities, these financial rate differences are taken to reflect economic cost differences. The surveys showed that the rate per ton-km on moving on a rough (earth) road was more than double the rate for a smooth asphalt road (about $0.50 per ton-km for the rough road, compared to $0.20 per ton-km on smooth roads). An interesting aspect of the case in Bangladesh was the realization that human–pulled vehicles need smooth surfaces even more than motor vehicles, and that road investments in black-topping could be justified when heavy NMT traffic exists, even though the number of motor vehicles in use is less than 50 per day. It was also clear that the people generally had small parcel loads or a few bags at a time to transport over short distances, which was best suited for the efficient form of NMT in Bangladesh (the rickshaw-van). Indeed, with road improvements there was a fast increase in both motor vehicles and NMT traffic. The Bangladesh studies also established that after road development there is dynamic growth in traffic and a change in vehicle composition: buses starting to appear for the first time, and overall traffic growth exceeded 100 percent even in the first year after project completion. The study also found that cost differences between the with- and without-project situations are best estimated through likely changes in the composition of vehicles (decline of bullock carts and head porterage, and increase in both NMT and motor vehicles) and related unit costs.

Source: (1) "Bangladesh Rural Infrastructure Impact Study," with special reference to RDP-7 and other projects, 1999. (2) Bangladesh Rural Infrastructure Strategy Study, 1996.

Savings due to Mode Changes (from NMT to motorized transport): Very significant savings can be made due to road improvement- or construction-induced changes in the modes of transport. Resulting cost reduction can ten fold as shown in Box 4.6 below.

Improved Valuation of Time Savings: A critical aspect of examining alternative RTI interventions is an understanding of the impact of improvements in infrastructure on journey times, and therefore (beyond the impact on vehicle operating costs) on productive time saved, including those associated with non-motorized travel and transit time of freight. The process of valuing time in transport operations is not without controversy (Box 4.7), and while there are currently no universally accepted methods for determining a "value of time," some general guidance is possible.[85] For additional, information on valuing travel time savings, see Gwilliam (1997).

Box 4.6. *Savings due to Mode Changes in Ghana and Elsewhere*

Studies in Ghana (and elsewhere) have established that head porterage takes about two person-days to move one ton-km, using factors of average load size, walking speed per hour, and time for the return trip (without load). Using the minimum wage rate, this amounted to about $2 to 2.50 per ton-km. The minimum wage is taken as a proxy for the resource costs (food, expenses, etc.), and for the time and effort involved.

More recent studies indicate that where transport is not available, the rural poor experience a shortage of productive time in doing various chores in their daily lives and farming, marketing, and transport activities, and therefore their time should be given a higher monetary value. This is indeed a valid consideration, but not reflected in the price noted above (see also next paragraph on the valuation of time savings). The estimated rate of $2 to 2.50 per ton-km mentioned above was also found to reflect the actual market charges for such operations.

This rate range is found valid for head porterage in many developing countries. In Balochistan (Pakistan), Nepal, and Bhutan, where mule transport is a common form of transport in rural areas, the actual cost is found to be about $3 to 4 per ton-km, including the cost of the mules and the persons walking with them. In Bhutan, a similar rate was found through market inquiries of actual charges levied, and also from indicative tariff rates published by the Royal Government of Bhutan. This rate should be compared with about $0.20 per ton-km for trucking operating costs on low-volume roads, which would become applicable after road construction or improvement.

Source: Adapted from Tampil Pankaj, 1991.

Box 4.7. *Valuing "Journey Time Saving" in Developing Countries*

The issue of valuing time, or more specifically journey time savings, has been the subject of extensive theoretical and empirical investigation. However, most of this work has focused on conventional journeys of people by road and reflects the traditional arguments of transport economics. These revolve around the use of resource assessments of value, or inferring resource values from the behavior of travelers. Walking trips and those by other non-motorized means of transport have largely been ignored. Moreover, debate has generally centered around the issue of valuing journeys in *working time or non-working time*. The first of these categories refers to time for which the traveler is paid out of employment remuneration, and the second to all other uses of time such as commuting, shopping or social purposes. These categorizations are appropriate to the economic and social structures of developed countries, yet they are less helpful when the study population comprises rural household members who are: (a) predominantly self-employed; and (b) characteristically engage in multi-purpose, or simultaneous task trips. The latter is especially true of women who in many societies are the dominant transporters at the household level (see Bryceson 1995).

Most transport economics literature assumes that the majority of the rural population in developing countries will be in non-wage employment, and it is therefore considered to be traveling in non-working time which is ascribed a zero value. This clearly does not make sense, either in resource or behavioral terms. Walking journeys consume both energy and time, which are both valuable resources in rural subsistence households. The creation of energy is rarely a free good. Moreover, there are numerous examples where the behavior of such societies indicates that they place a relatively high value on their time.

Source: Howe, 1997.

In collecting data on the value of time, special attention should be given to estimating values which can be applied to particular modes of travel, such as bus versus bicycle travel. In addition, overall journey length may change stated time values, as can income level. Both should be evaluated in survey data. Finally, time required for walking, waiting, or transfer may need to be valued differently than specific travel time (on or in vehicles) and should be reported separately where possible. Where it is not possible to obtain local values for travel time, estimates from household income or shadow wages should be substituted. Table 4.1 offers relevant guidelines:

Table 4.1. *The Valuation of Time Savings from Transport Improvements in Developing Countries*

Where it is not possible to derive values locally, the following bases should be used:
(W = wage rate per hour; H = household income per hour)

Trip Purpose	Rule	Value
Work trip	Cost to employer	1.33 w
Business	Cost to employer	1.33 w
Commuting and Other non-work	Empirically Observed value	0.3 H (adult) 0.15 H (child)
Walking/waiting	Empirically Observed value	1.5 x value for trip Purpose
Freight/Public Transport	Resource cost Approach	Vehicle time cost + driver age cost + occupants time

Source: Gwilliam, 1997.

Valuation of Social Benefits from Improved Access to Schools and Health Centers: It is often argued that the most important impacts of rural infrastructure improvements take place through changes in the patterns of personal mobility and increased social travel.[86] Improved rural access provides social benefits in promoting education, particularly through increased enrollment of girls, health benefits, increased labor mobility, the spread of information and knowledge, and also improved access to markets. Many studies demonstrate the dynamic changes that improved rural mobility brings to the social and economic life of rural areas. A study in Bangladesh comparing two sets of villages showed that villages with road access, compared with villages without access, fared much better in farm-gate price of produce, fertilizer use, land under irrigation, household income, income per acre of field crops, wage income of landless labor, and percentage of employed women.[87] Another comparative picture of villages from Bhutan, all under the same agro-climatic and cultural environment and also in the same district, not far from each other, demonstrate similarly impressive contrasts in school enrollment levels and other aspects (Table 4.2).

Table 4.2. *Access, Income, and Education in Bhutan*[88]

	"Accessible" (0-0.5 days walk to nearest road)	"Not accessible" (1-3 days walk to nearest road)
Distance to nearest road (walking time)	0-0.5	1-3
Average annual income/farm household	$176 equivalent	$71 equivalent
Enrollment of boys (age 6-16)	73%	42%
Enrollment of girls (age 6-16)	64%	22%

Source: Project Appraisal Document on a proposed credit to Bhutan for a rural access project, World Bank, November 1999.

One common approach to quantifying social benefits (particularly benefits from improved access to education and health facilities) is to use a sample case as guidance for assessing similar benefits from other roads improvements in similar areas or regions in the same country. Such estimates can be considered together with the usual transport cost savings estimated separately. However, care must be taken to ensure that there is no double-counting of benefits in the process. In the above study, benefits from education were estimated from increased school enrollment levels (due to improved access), using estimates of the incremental life earnings of the children who would have otherwise remained unskilled. Health benefits were assessed based on reduced sick days away from work, lost net income, and other health savings from better access to health centers. Such an approach may involve considerable field data collection and analysis. The first study along these lines for appraising a rural infrastructure investment was done recently for the Bhutan Rural Access Project which was approved by the Board of the World Bank in December 1999. The Bhutan case also highlights other important approaches for the careful assessment of benefits from rural road access improvements. These benefits include the estimation of mule-haulage costs in the without-project situation, and the use of a 40-year life assumption for the road, which specifically is defined as a well-designed and erosion-protected mountain road with a gravel surface with expected good maintenance (in the case of Bhutan). Sensitivity analysis regarding these assumptions was done (see Appendix E.2).

APPENDIX A
ROAD NETWORK, MOBILITY AND ACCESSIBILITY IN SELECTED COUNTRIES
(where available, data are 1998)

Country	Area	Pop.	Pop. Density	GDP per Capita	Main Road Network	Local Road Network	Total Road Network	Of which Paved	Road Density	Road Network/ Pop.	Road Asset Value (RAV)	RAV/ GDP	Maint. Exp./ Capita	Vehicle Ownership	Pers.-km	Pers.-km/ GDP	Access-ibility
(1)	(2)	(3)	(4)	(5)	(6)	(7)	(8)	(9)	(10)	(11)	(12)	(13)	(14)	(15)	(16)	(17)	(18)
	Thousand square km	Millions	Pop. per square km	$	Thousand km of national and regional/ state/ provincial roads	Thousand km of local government & community roads	Thousand km	Percent	Km of road per square km of land area	Km of roads per thousand persons	Billion $	Road Asset Value as % of GDP	Required vs. actual maintenance expenditure in $ per capita	Number of cars, buses and trucks per thousand persons	Km traveled per day per person; road and rail	Person-km divided by GDP in $	% of pop without all-season motorable road within 1-2 km of household
Low-Income																	
Burkina F.	274	11	39	243	10	6	16	12	0.06	1.5	2.1	79	5/1	5	0.8	1.2	17
Chad	1284	7	6	233	6	34	40	1	0.03	5.7	1.9	116	7/1	3	0.2	0.4	75
Ethiopia	1104	61	61	106	20	9	29	15	0.03	0.5	4.2	65	2/1	1	n.a.	n.a.	60
Ghana	239	19	81	405	15	23	38	24	0.16	2.0	3.5	45	5/2	7	n.a.	n.a.	20
Guinea	246	7	29	507	12	18	30	17	0.12	4.3	2.8	79	10/2	5	n.a.	n.a.	30
India	3288	980	330	439	1496	1823	3320	46	1.01	3.4	336	78	9/3	10	5.8	2.1	22
Nepal	147	23	160	210	5	7	13	31	0.09	0.6	1.0	21	1/0.5	3	0.2	0.3	40
Nigeria	924	121	133	343	63	73	136	27	0.15	1.1	14	34	3/0.2	11	4.1	2.9	10
Tanzania	945	32	36	249	28	60	88	4	0.09	2.8	6.8	85	5/2	4	n.a.	n.a.	30
Middle-Income																	
Brazil	8547	166	20	4691	265	1400	1665	10	0.20	10.0	161	21	20/14	76	15	1.2	9
Latvia	65	2	40	2667	20	39	59	39	0.91	29.5	12	226	120/34	241	n.a.	n.a.	3
Namibia	824	2	2	1824	14	50	64	8	0.08	32.0	8.5	233	85/21	78	n.a.	n.a.	30
Peru	1285	25	19	2528	17	57	74	12	0.06	3.0	11.4	18	9/3	118	9.7	1.4	25
Romania	238	23	98	1698	15	185	200	68	0.84	8.7	16.8	43	15/-	135	n.a.	n.a.	5
Russia	17075	147	9	1883	531	40	571	-	0.03	3.9	269	97	37/-	153	n.a.	n.a.	5
S. Africa	1221	41	34	3225	233	301	506	34	0.41	12.5	132	100	64/15	137	45	5.1*	20
Tunisia	164	9	60	2151	14	9	23	79	0.14	2.6	7.5	39	21/-	63	n.a.	n.a.	5
High-Income																	
Germany	349	82	235	26012	140	517	657	99	1.88	8.0	383	18	-/93	529	30	0.4	0
Japan	377	126	336	29926	187	965	1152	75	3.06	9.1	567	15	-/131	560	29	0.4	0
Sweden	412	9	21	20608	97	114	211	78	0.51	23.4	217	116	-/150	468	33	0.6	1
USA	9159	270	30	30449	1394	4954	6348	59	0.69	23.5	3779	46	-/101	780	55	0.7	1

* The unusually high ratio of person-kilometers per GDP in South Africa is related to the forced separation policies (and the resulting commuting needs) of apartheid.

Sources: Columns 2-5: World Bank, World Development Indicators Database. Columns 6-9, and 15-16: International Road Federation, World Road Statistics 2000, data 1994-98 (where available). Remaining columns: data from country-specific studies and own estimates and calculations. Column 12 (RAV): RAV was calculated as follows: (a) low-income countries: col. 6: $200,000/km, col. 7: $20,000/km; (b) middle-income countries: col. 6: $500,000/km, col. 7: $50,000/km; (c) high-income countries: col. 6: $2,000,000/km, col. 7: 200,000/km. Column 14: actual amounts are from IRF World Road Statistics or from World Bank project information; the required amounts were calculated as a percentage of the asset value, as follows: for low-income countries: 2.5% of RAV; for middle-income countries: 2.0% of RAV. Column 16 includes only movements by motorized means of transport. Column 18 represents rough estimates based on expert knowledge

APPENDIX B
DESIGNING BASIC ACCESS ROADS

General

This appendix provides guidance on the design of basic access roads.[89] Further guidance to the topic can be found in the literature.[90]

The design of motorized basic access necessitates a return to the guiding principles of highway engineering. Determining the minimum interventions necessary to ensure passability at least cost requires a thorough understanding of the complex interactions of soils, terrain, climate, and traffic. Moreover, creating sustainable solutions to the problems posed by these interactions requires a significant level of engineering judgment, technical skills, and local knowledge.

Standard solutions are often insufficient. Terrain conditions can vary considerably within countries and between regions. Traffic types and needs depend on the circumstances of individual communities. To achieve cost-effective basic access, it is important to tailor interventions to the specific situation and not to impose rigid designs. However, there are a number of basic engineering standards that should be adhered to, and these are summarized in Table B.1 below.

The supporting notes are not intended to present a comprehensive design procedure, but to supplement good engineering practices with low-cost solutions not normally included in conventional highway manuals.

Table B.1. *Basic Access Road Standards for Various Terrain*

Feature	Terrain		
	Flat	Rolling	Mountainous
Carriageway width	3.0 meters	2.5 to 3.0 meters	2.5 to 3.0 meters
	If shoulders are insufficient to allow passing of the prevailing vehicles, passing places of 20 meters length must be provided every 200 meters. Parking place for buses and trucks will be required in villages and towns.		
Formation width	3.5 to 5.0 meters	3.0 to 5.0 meters	3.0 to 4.0 meters
Minimum curve radius	12 meters	12 meters	8 meters
Road surface type (in-situ material unless otherwise stated)	Gravel on weak soils	Gravel or stone paving on steep sections or weak soils	Gravel or stone paving on steep sections or weak soils
Camber	5 to 8%	5 to 8%	3 to 5%
Maximum gradient	N/A	12%	12 to 15%
Water crossings	Concrete or stone drifts. 600mm diameter culverts. Vented fords for major crossings. Single-lane submersible or high-level bridges where water flow is substantial and perennial.		
Cross-sections and Side drains	Road required to be about 50 cm above flood level	Scour checks	Lined drains >10%

Source: Authors.

Soils

Only limited research has been carried out on the mechanisms that cause unpaved roads to become impassable.[91] This research has concluded that there is no significant correlation between soil characteristics and overall road passability. However, there does exist a significant correlation between passability and the adequacy of the drainage provision.

A significant percentage of a basic access road should be able to utilize the existing in-situ soils. However some soils, even if well compacted and drained, are still too weak to resist shearing under the intended traffic load, or may be too slippery for steep gradients (for example, black cotton soils).

The following thresholds are therefore proposed, below which motorized roads should be provided with a gravel or similar running surface:

- In-situ materials should demonstrate a minimum California Bearing Ratio (CBR) of 15 percent at prevailing moisture conditions.[92]

- In areas other than flat terrain, the shrinkage product (SP)[93] of the surface material should not exceed 365.

Based on international experience with soil types, the following guidelines (Box B.1) can be considered for preliminary appraisal. However, the findings should be carefully scrutinized at the design stage.

Box B.1 *Design Considerations for Different Soil Conditions*

Laterite—In general, lateritic soils can be successfully used for the formation of low-volume traffic roads. If the material is close to a mechanically stable particle-size distribution, then it performs well as a surface material for low-volume traffic roads. Soil of this quality frequently occurs in-situ and hence, gravelling is not required. Suitable rock for crushed aggregate is often scarce in tropical areas where weathering is usually intense and lateritic gravel is normally used instead. The clay and silt content is often high and as a consequence, makes the road surface slippery during rains. Temporary closing of laterite roads during rainfalls is advisable.

Tropical alluvial—In general, alluvial soils can also be used for the formation of low-volume traffic roads. In principle, alluvial soil makes a good surface material. However, alluvial deposits are normally stratified with a uniform particle size in the single stratum. It is therefore necessary to mix layers with different grain sizes to achieve a well-graded gravel.

Volcanic ash—Ash soils in areas of persistent high volcanic activity are highly sensitive to disturbance and therefore should not be use for road construction. In areas where the annual cycle includes hot dry seasons, ash soils transform into halloysitic soils (commonly called "red coffee" soil). Low-traffic roads can be constructed using this soil. However, the material becomes very slippery during rains and if the road is not gravelled, it might be advisable to close the road during rainfalls. Over-compacting of halloysitic soils should be avoided as this makes the soils weaker and more susceptible to the effect of moisture.

Expansive clays—Using expansive clays to build roads in temperate climates poses few problems. A gravel surface needs to be added onto a well-draining camber to avoid penetration of surface water into the formation material. In tropical climates, black cotton sections should be avoided as much as possible.

continued...

> **...Box B.1 continued**
>
> Where this is not possible, it is advisable to raise the road above the surrounding level and to provide wide and shallow ditches. Two layers of compacted gravel surface are required. In addition, the shoulders should be covered (haunched) with the gravel course in order to avoid any rainwater penetrating the surface and weakening the formation material. Expansive soils in tropical climates can severely erode if adequate protection measures are not taken, especially in ditches with slopes greater than 2 percent, culvert outlets and embankment slopes.
>
> *Desert soils*—Wind-blown sands dominate and are often single-sized material, which makes it difficult to compact. At the same time, there is hardly sufficient water available for effective compaction. Sand alone should not be used as road-surface material and needs to be sealed or covered with an adequate surface material, such as seal, gravel, or calcrete. It is often difficult to find suitable gravel as surface material. Calcrete has been tried in a number of cases (such as Botswana, Namibia) with good results, but can be difficult to extract by labor-based methods.
>
> *Source:* Authors.

Terrain

The terrain through which a road or track leads can conveniently be classified as flat, rolling, or mountainous, defined by both subjective descriptions and average ground slope.[94] The terrain type has considerable impact on the nature of the drainage, alignment, road structure, performance after construction, and ultimately, costs.

Recommendations for basic standards applicable to each terrain category are set out below for rolling terrain, very flat, and very steep conditions.

Rolling Terrain: Rolling terrain is the most commonly encountered terrain type. Whereas existing tracks in this terrain are normally motorable for the majority of their length, there often are distinct problem areas that make access difficult. Bearing-capacity problems are more prevalent on level sections or shallow grades, while slipperiness problems tend to occur on steeper grades. These sections need careful inspection in determining where imported soils or gravel surfacing are required.

Typically, the existing alignment will have developed naturally over time to connect villages by the most direct route, possibly following non-motorized transport routes that avoid minor obstacles. Therefore, it may be necessary to realign short sections to avoid steep grades and overly tight curves for motorized traffic. However, finding an alternative alignment is relatively straightforward in this terrain.

Drainage provision is the most important aspect, and all existing cross-drainage points will require inspection and treatment. The solution may be as simple as a stone-surfaced "splash," but work must always be done to ensure that the road is not cut by erosion as a consequence of heavy runoff. Up to five splashes, drifts, or culverts may be required in a typical kilometer of road. All structures and drainage outlets must be securely protected against erosion.

Runoff from the road surface must be quickly diverted to adjacent land to avoid ponding and softening. This may not require side drains throughout, but the road surface must be correctly shaped with adequate camber or cross slopes. Although 5 percent is usually specified for engineered roads, 8 percent has been found to perform better on low-traffic earth and gravel roads.

Where side ditches are provided, they must be equipped with scour checks if the gradient exceeds 4 percent and mitre drains every 20 meters to protect against erosion (Figure B.1).

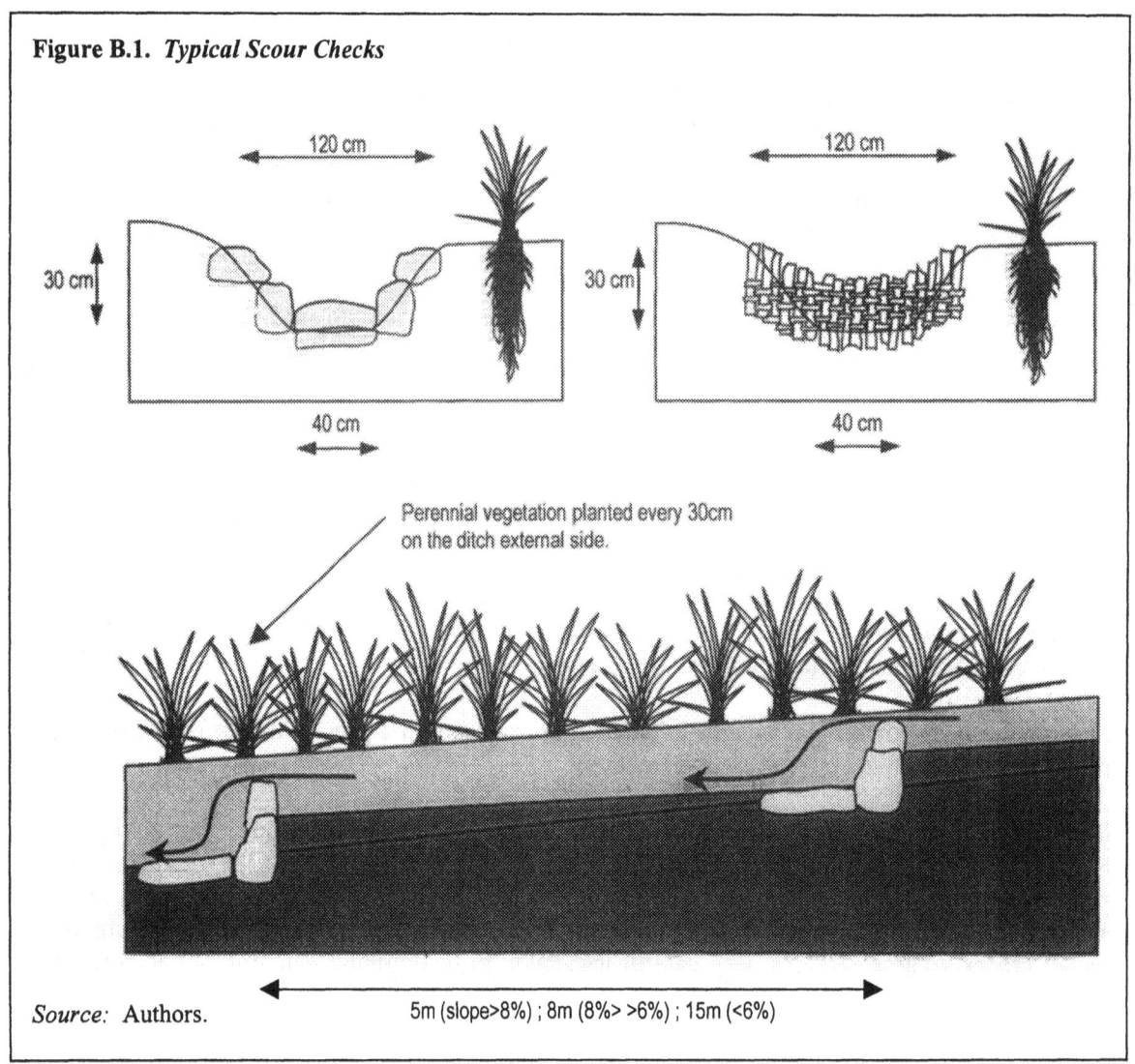

Figure B.1. *Typical Scour Checks*

Source: Authors.

Basic access roads in rolling terrain are single lane with a carriageway width between 2.5 and 3 meters. The total formation width should be between 3 and 5 meters. The wider formation allows light vehicles to pass at low speeds if the shoulder can be driven on.

However, sufficient passing places (bypasses) at suitable places (minimum every 200 meters) have to be provided. The width of the carriageway at these passing places should be at least 5 meters. The length of the passing places must be a minimum of 20 meters.

The absolute minimum horizontal radius for curves is 12 meters. This is just within the minimum turning radius of small commercial vehicles and buses. If much larger vehicles are expected and required, the road geometry must be amended accordingly, but this would not normally be expected on basic access roads. The most important issue is to ensure that the geometry is consistent. Long, straight sections and shallow high-speed curves must not be followed by unmarked tight curves. This would be hazardous for motorized traffic, and even more so for the pedestrians they may encounter.

The longitudinal gradient should not exceed 12 percent. Sections with a gradient greater than 10 percent should always be gravelled and possibly be considered for paving (see alternative pavement options in chapter 4 of this appendix). It may be necessary to gravel more shallow gradients depending on the erosion-resistance properties of the in-situ soil. This can only be determined by on-site inspection.

Typical cross sections for improvement work are shown in Figure B.2 below. Where side slopes are greater than 4 percent, it is only necessary to provide side drains on one side of the road.

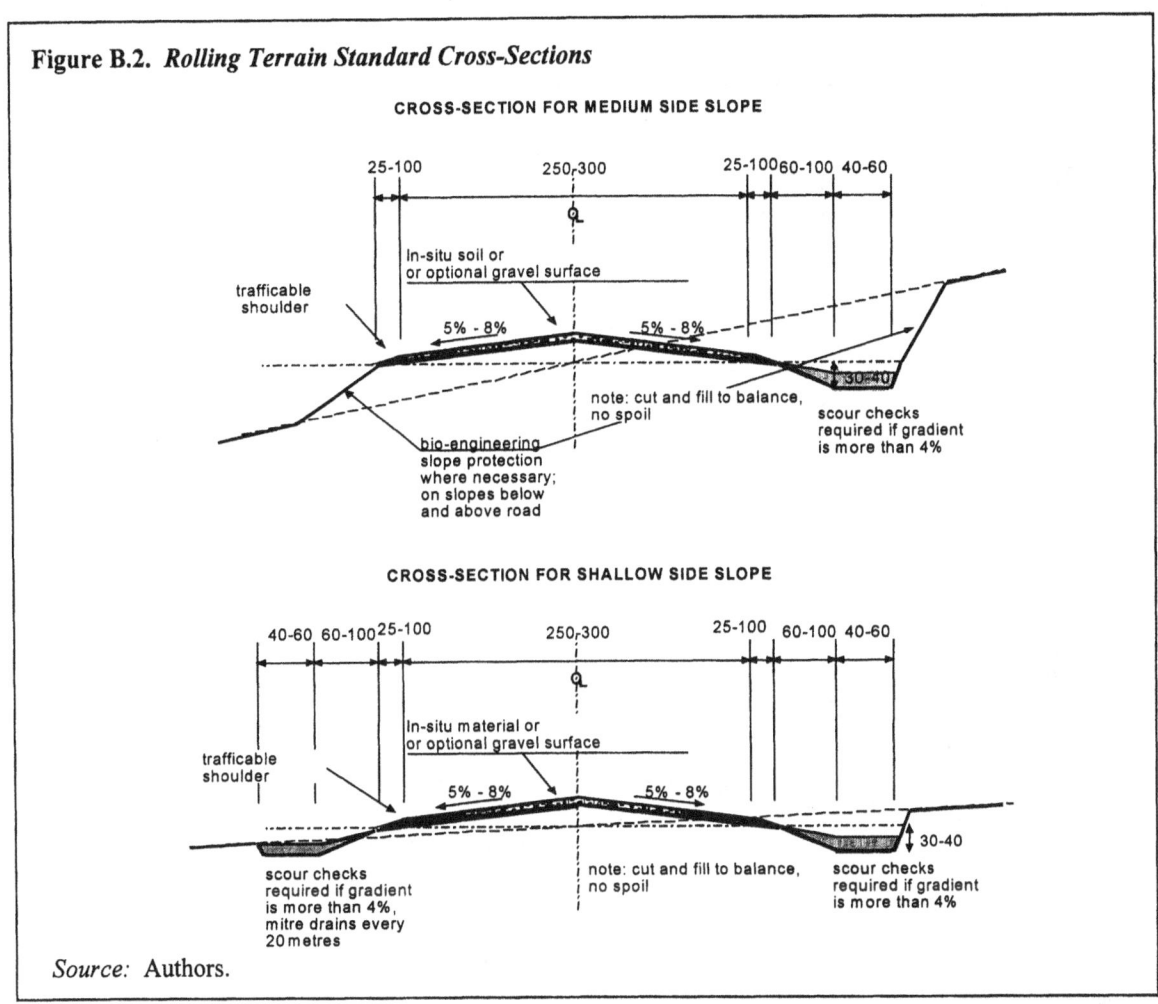

Figure B.2. *Rolling Terrain Standard Cross-Sections*

Source: Authors.

Flat Terrain: The location of existing tracks on flat terrain can be very seasonal. Traffic tends to take the most direct line in dry periods, and circumvent trouble spots as they occur in the wet season. Before a fixed route is established, it is essential to carefully study the drainage patterns and quantify the impact. Even relatively minor works can create a dam with associated erosion in periods of high rainfall. Drainage structures must be sufficient to ensure that flood flows can pass unimpeded. This may require submersible structures for areas with short flood periods, but require high-level bridges in areas with significant flooding.

In low-rainfall areas, the typical cross-section is similar to that of rolling terrain. However, in high rainfall areas it is necessary to elevate the road above flood level to maintain access. A freeboard of 0.5 meters above flood level is usually sufficient to ensure that the road surface does not lose its strength. Material can be used from adjacent land, but such embankments usually need surfacing with imported material. In these circumstances, spot improvement is not a feasible option.

Embankment widths may be up to 6.5 meters, which is wider than that applied in rolling terrain, to allow for possible softening of the edges during flood conditions. A minimum gradient of 1 percent should be applied, if possible, to all side drainage to avoid ponding. In seasonally flooded areas however, side drains have limited usefulness. A typical embankment section is shown in Figure B.3 below. Since the natural material may be highly erodible, building protection with natural materials becomes a priority activity. The embankment slope must be matched to the stable angle of the prevailing material.

Material for the embankment should not be excavated directly along the embankment foot, as this allows water to penetrate the fill. Borrow-areas or trenches should be located at some distance from the embankment (10 meters). These borrow-areas should be excavated to be as shallow as possible, and after the construction, they should be reinstated (slopes made shallow, topsoil brought back and vegetation planted). In agricultural areas, excavation planning should be carried out in participation with farmers to optimize location and methods. This will also ensure that the borrow places are best utilized (such as, for fish ponds, rice paddies, and so forth).

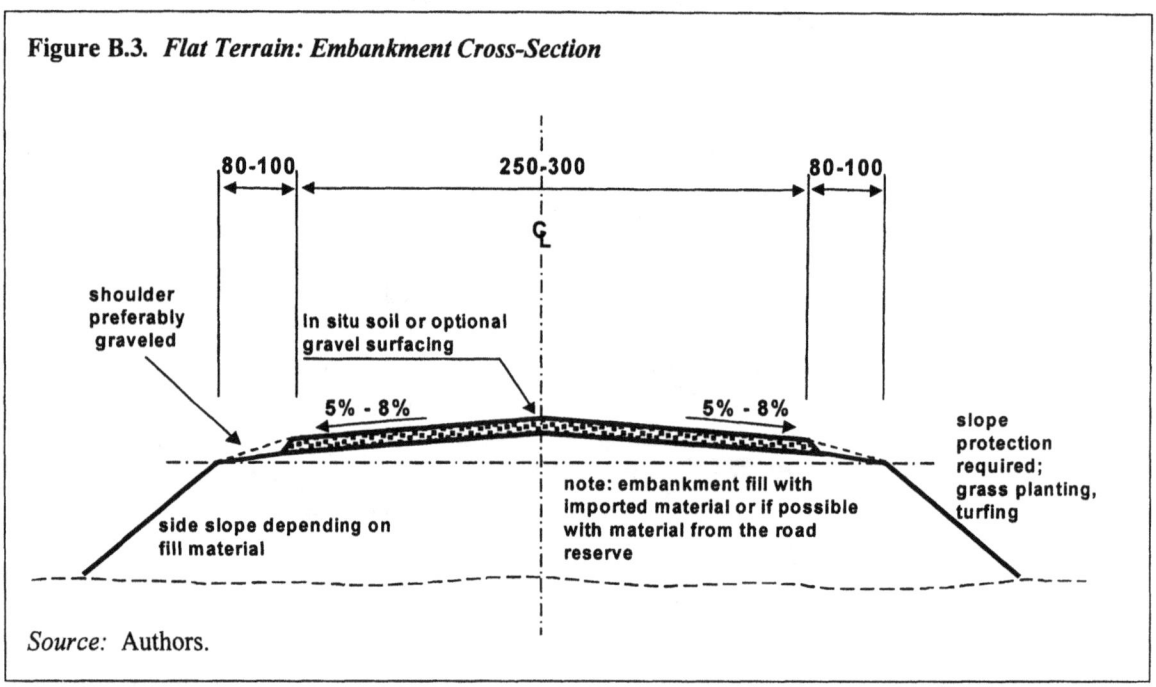

Figure B.3. *Flat Terrain: Embankment Cross-Section*

Source: Authors.

Expansive clays, often termed black cotton, present a formidable problem that will always need special treatment (expansive clays occur in all terrain types, but are more prevalent and difficult to circumvent in flat terrain). For low-traffic levels, the cross-section shown in Figure B.4, below, usually provides sufficient strength.

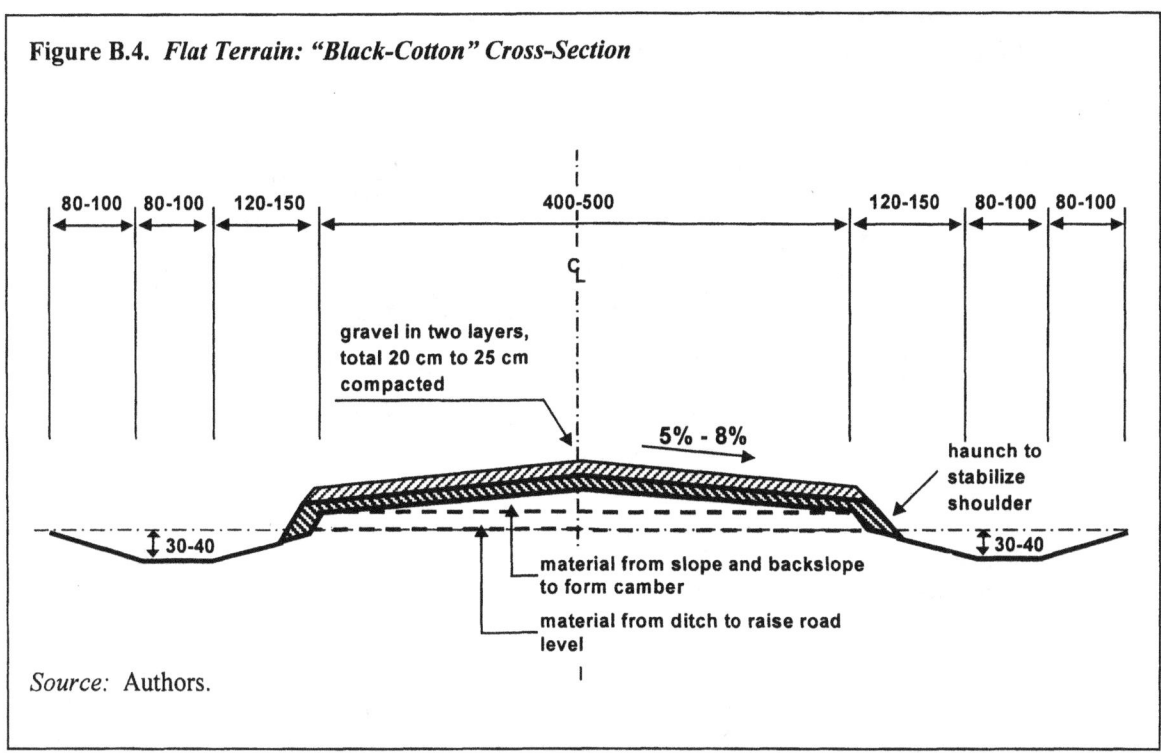

Figure B.4. *Flat Terrain: "Black-Cotton" Cross-Section*

Source: Authors.

Mountainous Terrain: Existing tracks in hilly and mountainous terrain have usually evolved along foot or pack animal trails. Common risks include excessive gradients and tight curves on hairpin bends, causing vehicles to carry out reversing maneuvers in dangerous circumstances. A significant amount of realignment can be expected in this terrain, requiring a full reconnaissance of alternative routes. However, it is possible for experienced surveyors to determine adequate routes by field survey using handheld instruments (such as GPS, abney level).

To minimize the costs associated with designing basic roads for this terrain, standards may be reduced to the absolute minimum in terms of road width and maximum gradients. However, the road must remain passable to the typical traffic in the area. The minimal standard for a single lane would be a carriageway width of 2.5 meters. Total formation width should be between 3.0 and 4.0 meters.

Sufficient passing places at suitable sites should be provided. The minimum spacing should be 200 meters, or more frequently where vision is restricted. Carriageway width and length at the passing places should be a minimum of 5.0 and 20.0 meters, respectively.

The absolute minimum horizontal radius for curves is 8.0 meters. Widening the curves may also be required to increase the visibility of oncoming traffic. This is a particular problem where steep-cut faces restrict sight distance. The curve widening should be between 1.0 and 2.0 meters depending on the nature of the curve and site conditions. The maximum gradient in curves should not exceed 5 percent.

In general, the maximum gradient should not exceed 15 percent. Sections with a gradient greater than 10 percent should be considered for paving (see alternative pavement options in chapter 4 of this appendix). Hairpin bends need to be carefully set out with respect to both curvature and gradients to ensure that the anticipated traffic can negotiate them without danger (Figure B.5).

Figure B.5. *Mountainous Terrain: Construction of Hairpin Bends*

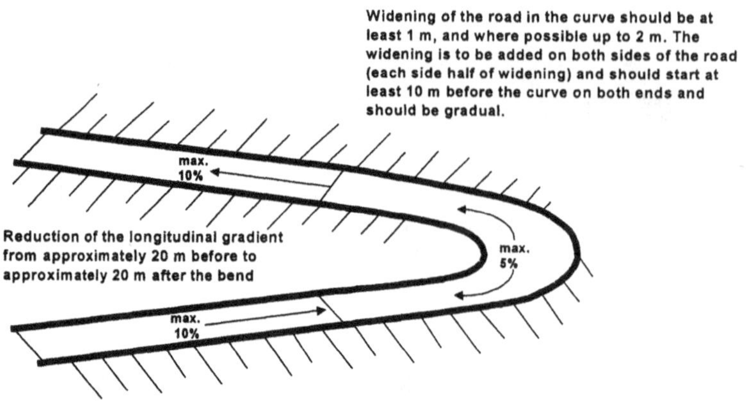

Source: "Low Cost Road Construction in Indonesia, Labor-Based Road Projects in Manggarai District, Volume 1, Intercooperation," by A. Beusch, P. Hartmann, R.C. Petts, P. Winkelmann.

Special attention must be paid to slope stability. Existing alignments are usually fairly stable, and problem areas are obvious. However, new alignments can precipitate slip failure on uphill cut-faces, and create severe erosion problems downstream of drainage outlets. Considerable care must be taken with stabilization measures. Even relatively small landslides can block these small mountain roads. The TRL guidelines on mountain roads contains a considerable amount of information in this area.[95]

Bio-engineering approaches, utilizing appropriate plants to solve structural and environmental problems, have proven very cost-effective in recent projects in Nepal. These sustainable methods are both labor-intensive and replicable for rural areas (see Chapter 6 of this appendix).

Retaining walls are required on both the valley and mountain side depending on the stability of the material, especially where vegetation cannot stabilize the slopes (Figure B.6). Retaining walls should be constructed using dry masonry for heights up to 4 meters and gabion walls for heights above 4 meters or where there is increased earth pressure. Cement-bound masonry should only be used where absolutely necessary.

Figure B.6. *Mountainous Terrain: The Construction of Retaining Walls*

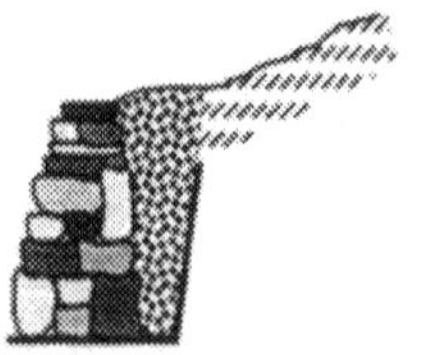

- dry stone retaining walls for heights up to 4 m
- crown width minimum 1 m
- slope face 3:1
- stone filter at back of wall
- weep holes 20 cm above ground, at every 2 m to 3 m

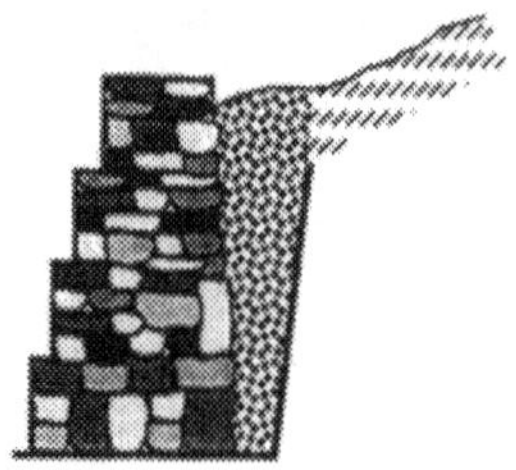

- gabion retaining walls for heights more
- stone filter at back of wall (check design details and dimensions in relevant manuals)

Source: Authors.

Drainage structures can be similar to those adopted in rolling terrain. Protection of the outfalls is critical and may need to be taken well beyond the road reserve, possibly for the entire drop to the valley floor. Gully erosion related to drainage outfalls is causing severe environmental damage in many rural areas.

Two typical mountain road cross-sections are shown in Figure B.7 below. These use alternative approaches to the problem of dealing with drainage and minimizing costs. Advantages and disadvantages of the two approaches are given.

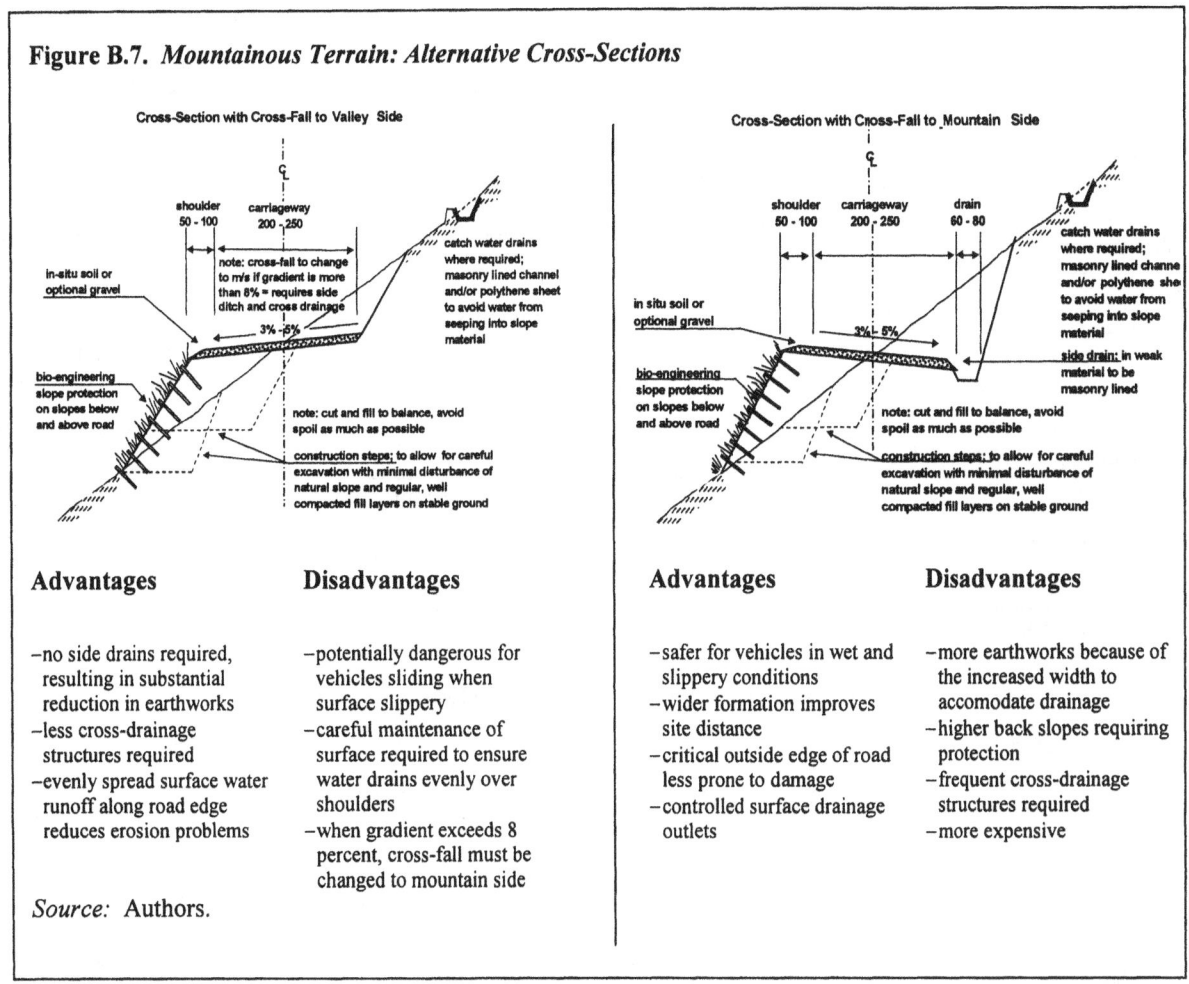

Figure B.7. *Mountainous Terrain: Alternative Cross-Sections*

Cross-Section with Cross-Fall to Valley Side

Advantages
- no side drains required, resulting in substantial reduction in earthworks
- less cross-drainage structures required
- evenly spread surface water runoff along road edge reduces erosion problems

Disadvantages
- potentially dangerous for vehicles sliding when surface slippery
- careful maintenance of surface required to ensure water drains evenly over shoulders
- when gradient exceeds 8 percent, cross-fall must be changed to mountain side

Source: Authors.

Cross-Section with Cross-Fall to Mountain Side

Advantages
- safer for vehicles in wet and slippery conditions
- wider formation improves site distance
- critical outside edge of road less prone to damage
- controlled surface drainage outlets

Disadvantages
- more earthworks because of the increased width to accomodate drainage
- higher back slopes requiring protection
- frequent cross-drainage structures required
- more expensive

Alternative Pavement Options

Alternative pavement types may be required for roads or road sections where the in-situ material or gravel does not provide the required quality surface. This may be the case on steep sections exceeding 10 percent, sections passing villages, or simply where the in-situ soils are too weak and gravel is not available or too expensive. Some of the available options for paving are discussed in Box B.2.

Box B.2. *Paving Options*

Stone Paving (see also Figure B.8)

Description	Natural stones measuring no more than 20 to 30 cm are laid on a 5 cm sand/gravel bed with the top surface set to the final cross-fall. The large stones are set with the wider face to the bottom. Empty spaces are filled with smaller stones and firmly wedged into place. Compaction is carried out with a vibrating pedestrian roller. The surface is then sealed with a gravel-sand-clay mixture and the finished paving is compacted again.
Uses	• Surface for low-traffic roads • Base for urban roads • Base for low-traffic roads which would require upgrading to asphalt standard if the traffic level is likely to increase beyond the economical threshold of gravel and stone-paved roads
Characteristics	• Labor-based construction method • Use of locally occurring materials • Ease of maintenance
Traffic	• For low-volume roads as surface • All traffic categories as a base
Cost	Comparable with gravel surfacing if stones occur in road locality
Life	Stone paving can have a very long life if maintained properly. Resealing should be done an average of every three years. Stones broken out of the pavement or damaged edges should be replaced immediately in order to avoid costly repairs

Clay or Concrete Brick Paving

Description	Burnt clay or concrete brick (200 x 100 x 80 mm approximately) laid on a thin layer (about 4 cm) of clean sand, on a conventional road base.
Uses	• Surface for low-traffic roads, especially short sections • Surface for urban roads, where speeds are below 50 km/h
Characteristics	• Labor-based construction method • High load-carrying capacity • Reusable surfacing and can have high local resources component • Ease of maintenance
Traffic	• For low volume as surface for short sections • From residential streets to heavy industrial application
Cost	Competitive with asphalt concrete in Europe where labor costs are high. Potential for significant cost savings in developing countries.
Life	Initial life 20 years and more, reusable bricks and blocks

Bituminous Surface Dressing

Description	A thin film of bitumen applied mechanically or by hand onto the road surface and covered with a layer of stone chipping, then lightly rolled.
Uses	• Surface for low-traffic roads and for short sections • Surface for urban roads (Multiple coats may be applied if circumstances warrant)
Characteristics	• Permits labor-based construction method • Provides durable dust-free running surface • Provides waterproof pavement seal and arrests surface deterioration • Allows for ease of maintenance
Traffic	• Can be used for all traffic categories
Cost	Inexpensive: typically 25% of the cost of an asphalt concrete surfacing. On average $1 to $2 per square meter and coat.
Life	Typically five to 15 years in a tropical environment

Source: Authors.

Slurry seal, hand-mixed asphalt, and stone sets are additional options that also may be applicable for very-low-volume situations where gravel is scarce.

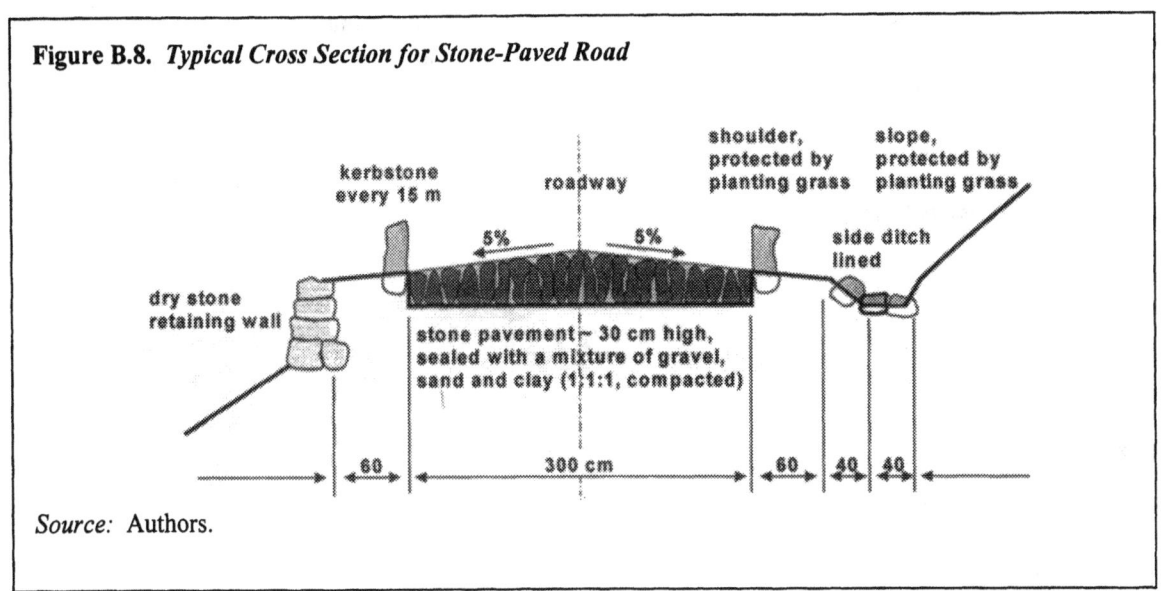

Figure B.8. *Typical Cross Section for Stone-Paved Road*

Source: Authors.

Water Crossings

Water crossings are the most essential and potentially the most expensive intervention to secure basic access. The conventional solution is usually a clear-span low-maintenance structure of steel or reinforced concrete on substantial abutments for river crossings, and pre-cast concrete pipes or box culverts for lower flows, designed to accommodate flood flows under all conditions other than exceptional events.[96] However, this is often not an affordable solution and for basic access, it is necessary to explore other options.

One option is the use of timber bridges on masonry, gabion, or reinforced earth abutments. This provides considerable savings on initial costs and maximizes the use of local skills and resources. However, it is only viable where suitable timber is readily available and spans are usually limited to six meters. There is also the likelihood of high maintenance costs and a short life span if the timber is not insect- and rot-resistant (either naturally or through special treatments).

Another option is to build a structure that can easily be overtopped without damage. These options include drifts and vented drifts. The decision should be based on flow patterns and community usage. Small rivers and streams in tropical regions are often wet-weather flow only, and high-flood levels are of short duration. A simple drift is usually adequate to secure vehicle access in these circumstances. For continuous flows, vented drifts can be designed to pass normal discharge, only submerging during floods.

It must be remembered that foot and non-motorized traffic constitute a significant portion of the traffic on basic access roads. Consideration should be given to providing safe passage for pedestrian and bicycle traffic. On long single-lane bridges, railings and a one-side elevated foot and bicycle path should be considered. Where submersible structures are frequently and deeply submerged, the provision of a separate low-cost footbridge might be considered.

Thorough site investigations and hydraulic design are necessary not only for large structures but also for relatively small structures on low-volume traffic roads. Figure B.9 shows some options for drainage structures appropriate for labor-intensive implementation by small-scale or community contracts. Their design needs to be adapted to the local conditions, including locally available materials and skills.

Drifts: These are the simplest structures available and are easy to maintain. They can be built of stone or concrete. Care should be taken to ensure that they are not scoured by the drainage flow. They must also be shaped to avoid damage to low ground-clearance vehicles.

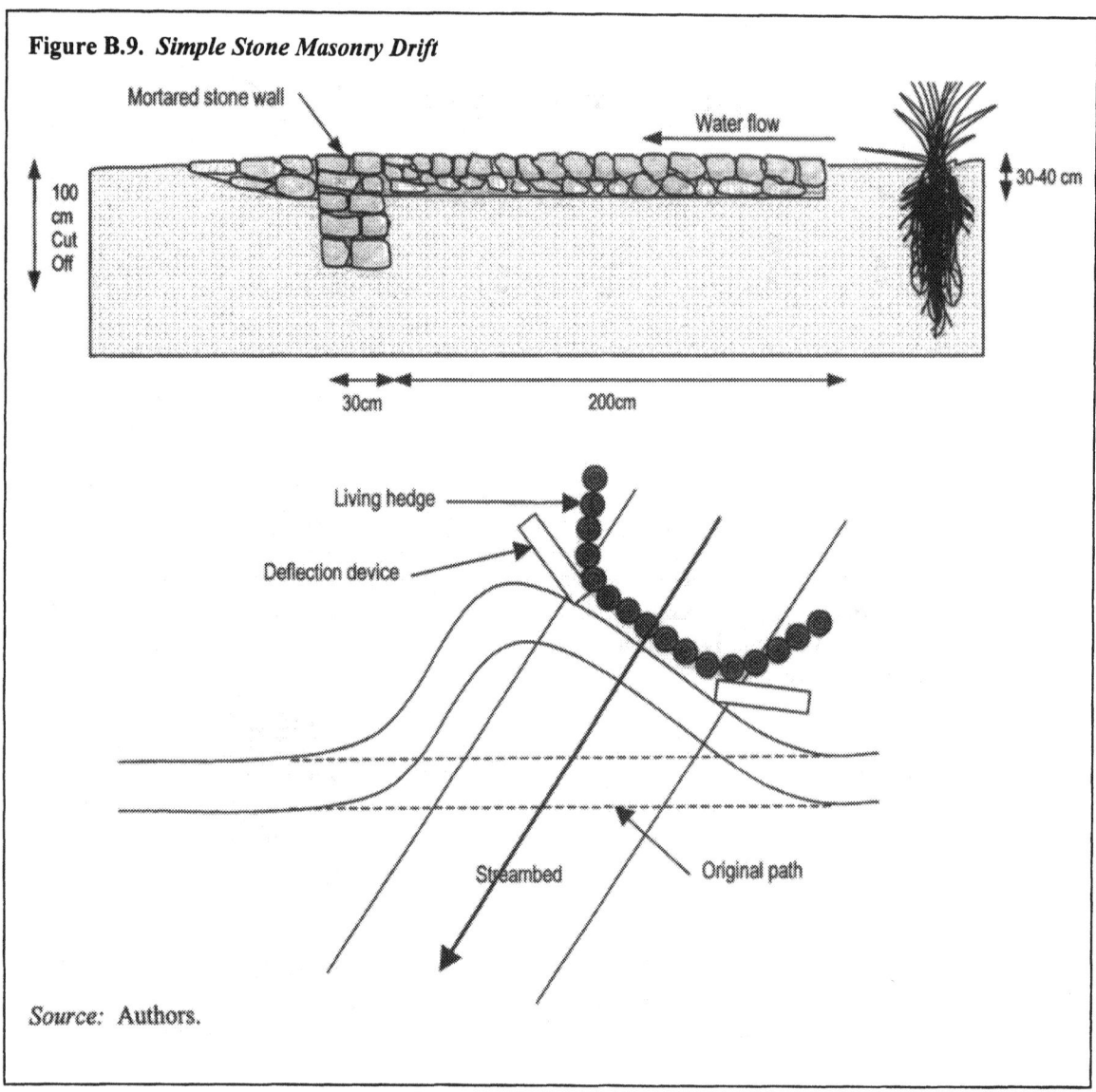

Vented Drifts: Vented drifts allow dry passage in periods of low flow, but act as drifts in periods of high flow. It is important to ensure that the structures are well anchored to the streambed, as there can be significant uplift when partly submerged. They are also easily blocked by debris and require attention after every flood. A downstream scour apron is also essential.

In some situations, flood levels may be very high. Flood posts must be provided to indicate water levels to prospective traffic. There are many recorded cases of fatal accidents in these situations. A very simple vented drift is shown in Figure B.10 below, where masonry arch culverts are combined with a masonry drift "overflow."

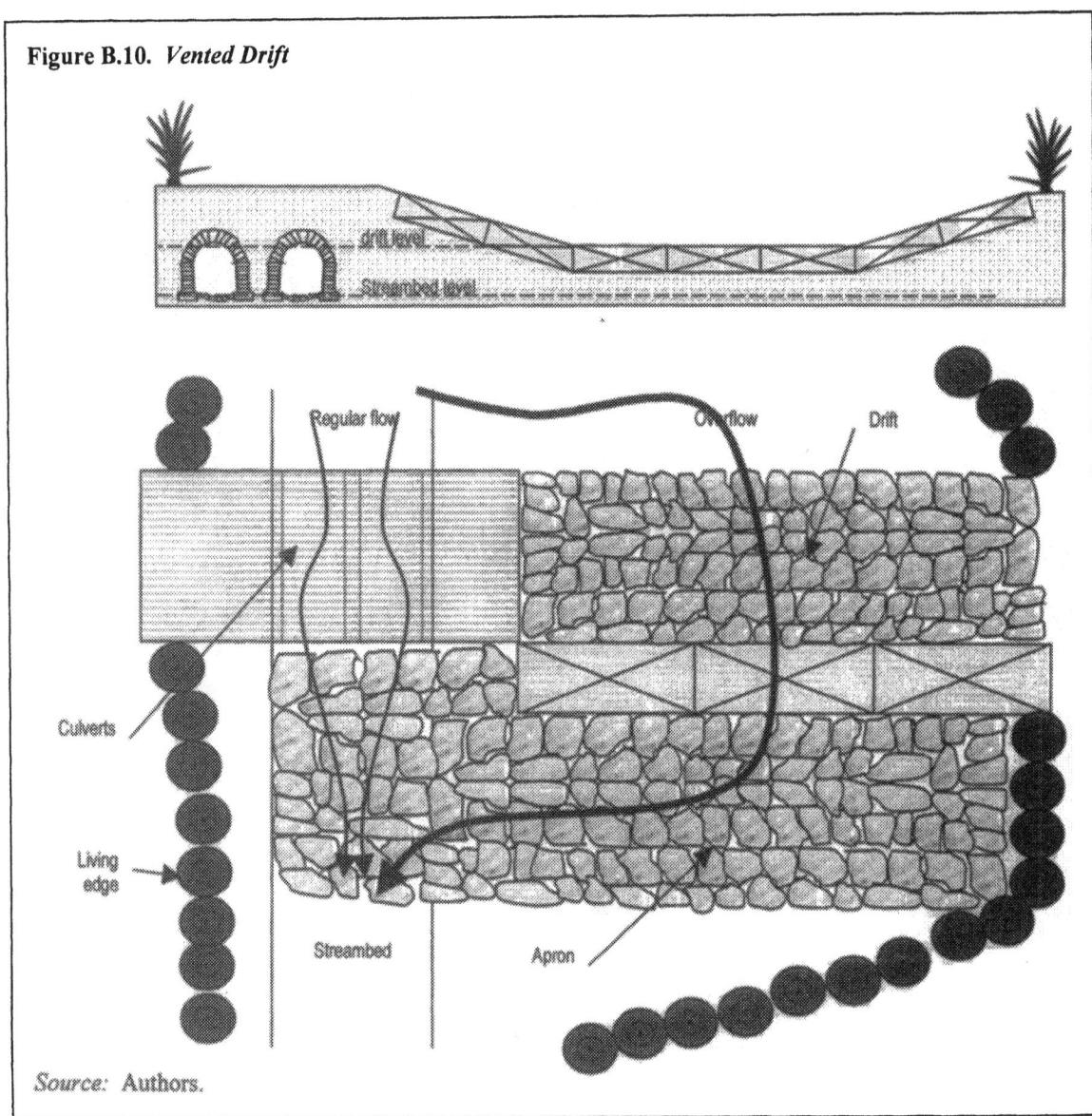

Figure B.10. *Vented Drift*

Source: Authors.

Multiple Culverts

The conventional solution to cross-drainage is the provision of culverts, usually made from prefabricated reinforced concrete or proprietary galvanized steel systems such as Armco. Large-diameter culverts are available that are capable of passing high discharges. However, such items are relatively expensive, difficult to handle without specialized equipment, and may require significant earthworks—out of proportion to the scale of work for basic access provision.

The alternative for basic access is the construction of unreinforced concrete pipes on site or the construction of small masonry arches. The minimum diameter should be 60 cm to ensure they can be cleaned. Such items can be installed in multiple lines to cope with larger flows.

Figure B.11 illustrates a labor-intensive procedure for the production of masonry arches.

Figure B.11. *The Construction of Masonry Arch Culverts*

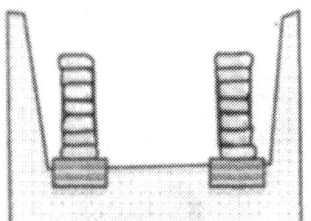
Step 1: after removing natural soil, foundations are set in place and lateral stone walls built.

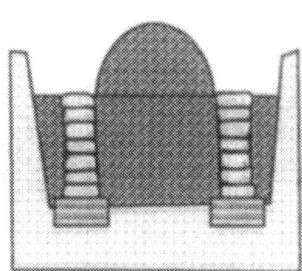
Step 2: soil is compacted on both sides of the walls. An arch-shaped earth volume is created on top of it.

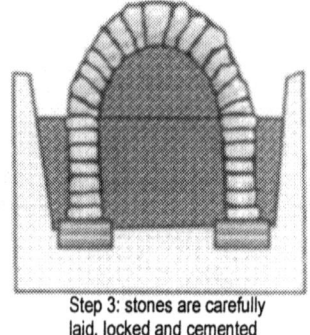
Step 3: stones are carefully laid, locked and cemented around the earth arch.

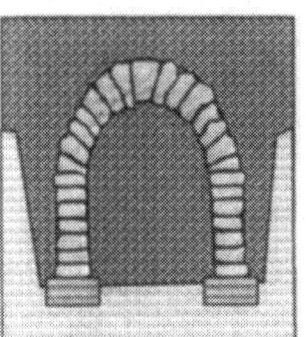
Step 4: the final earth layer is laid and compacted on top of the stone arch up to the carriageway level.

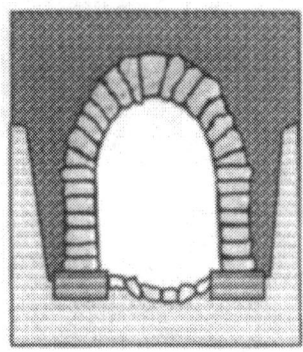
Step 5: compacted soil within the culvert is removed through openings. A stone layer is put at the bottom and extended as aprons.

Source: Authors.

Bridges: Timber framework and masonry arch bridges provide a local solution that requires only limited equipment and local materials. Both masonry arch and timber framework bridges require artisan skills that are usually not available. In the context of large-scale labor-based bridge construction, it might prove cost-effective to build capacity by training local artisans.

The design life of timber varies from five years for untreated softwood to 20 years for hardwood timber. Treatment with chemical preservatives can extend the design life considerably. To be effective, treatment should take place in a pressuring device. An alternative is "hot and cold treatment" with creosote. Brush or spray treatments will provide only temporary protection.

Figure B.12 below, represents the most rudimentary wooden bridge, suitable for relatively low flows and light traffic. More sophisticated structures would involve piled abutments, sawn deck beams, and running boards.

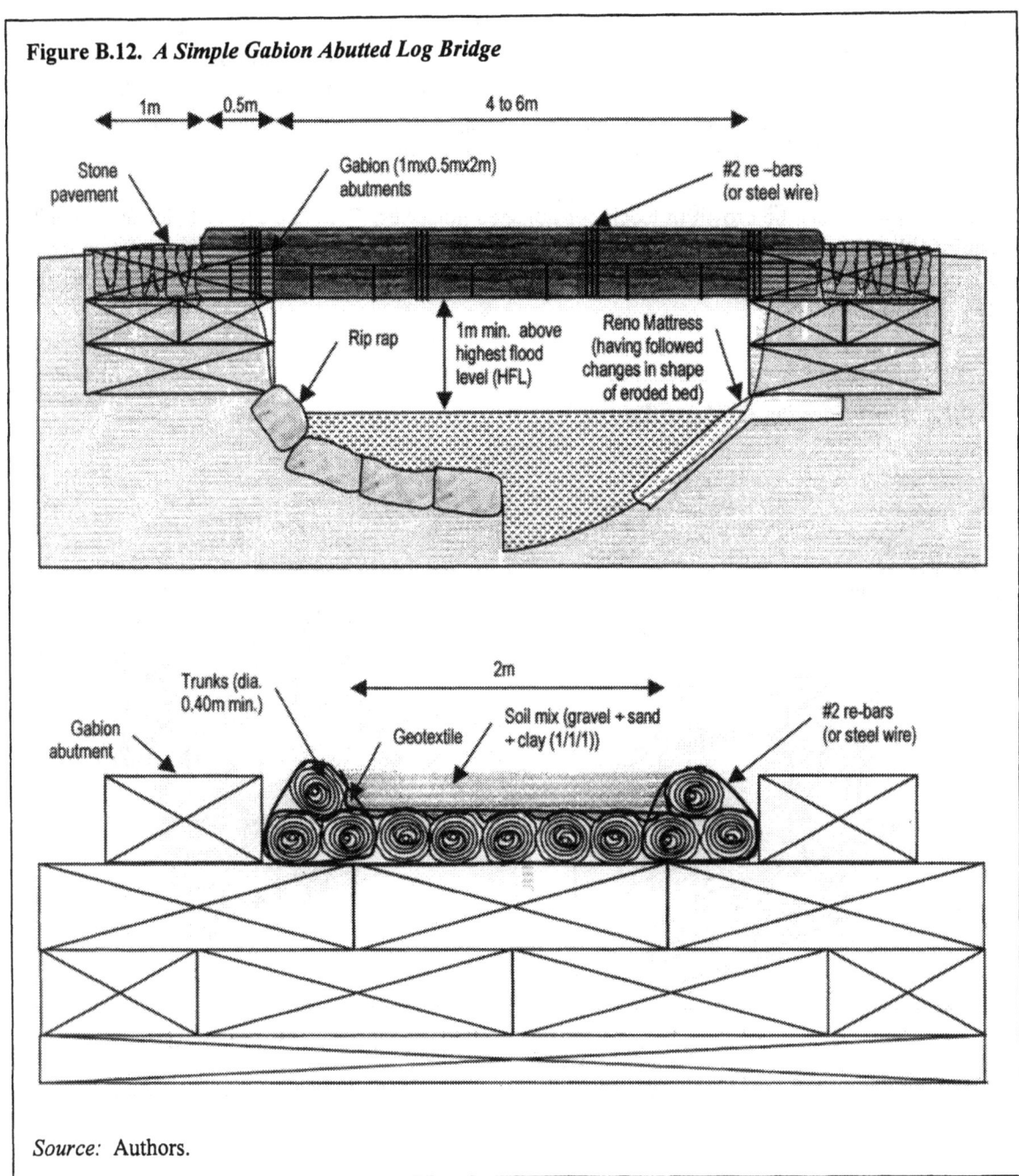

Figure B.12. *A Simple Gabion Abutted Log Bridge*

Source: Authors.

Bio-engineering

The major threat to the sustainability of low-cost earth and gravel roads is the erosive effect of water, in particular the scouring of side drains, drainage outfalls, road and embankment edges, and exposed slopes in cuts. Traditionally, it has been considered sufficient to rely on the eventual reestablishment of natural vegetation, or to encourage its growth by turfing. This rarely results in the best type of plant to resist erosion, however, with species that destroy carriageways and are not removed by maintenance workers. Alternatively, masonry and concrete check structures may be constructed—but these are expensive and often aggravate the situation.

Innovative work in several countries, but particularly Nepal[97] and the Caribbean islands, has demonstrated that it is possible to select and utilize particular combinations of plant species to provide sound engineering solutions. A common example is Vetiver grass,[98] which is used to stabilize terraces and gullies. Likewise, trees, shrubs, and other grasses may be used to stabilize slopes, protect embankments, and provide live check structures in drains.[99]

Suitable plant species can be grown in locally established nurseries. Works are very labor-intensive and require little capital investment. Skills developed may be useful in the community for other conservation projects. Some examples of the bio-engineered solutions to slope stability are given in Figures B.13 and B.14.

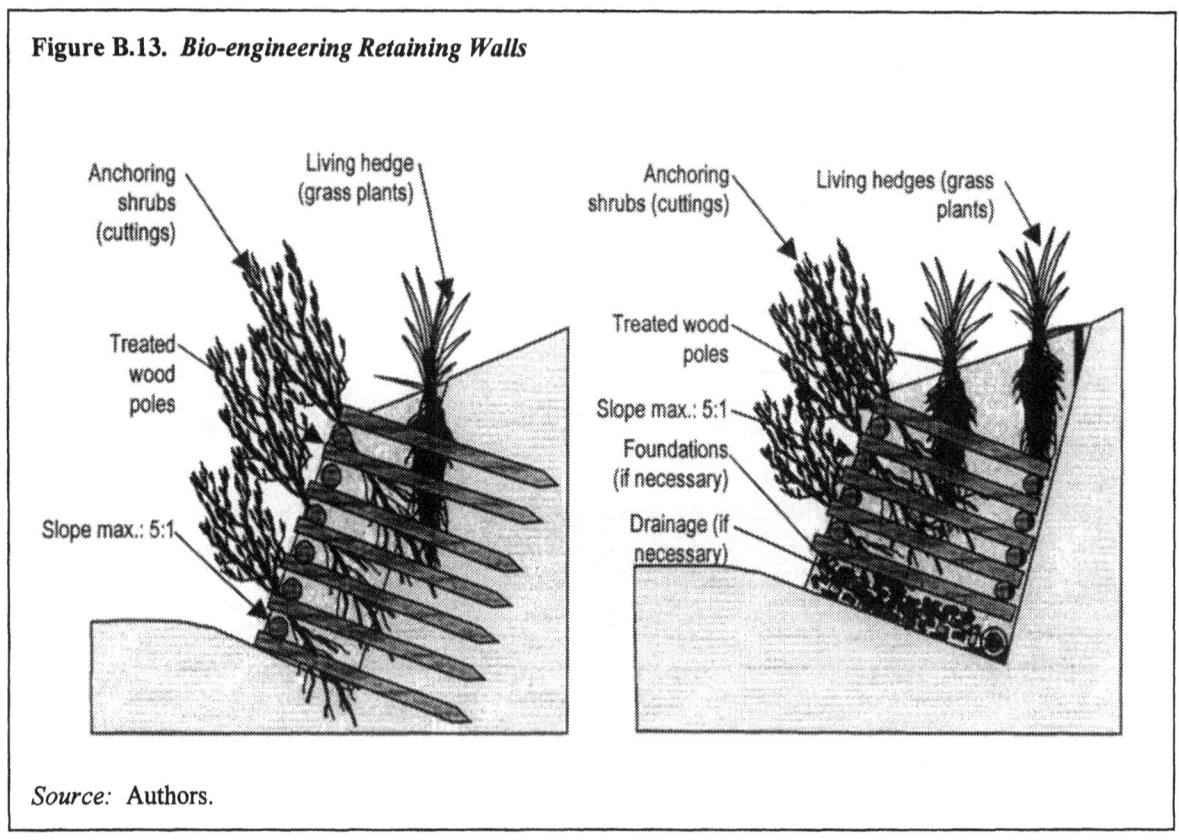

Figure B.13. *Bio-engineering Retaining Walls*

Source: Authors.

Wood "cages" are a temporary solution and their anti-erosion and anchoring functions will be performed by the plants as they become established. Dense grass hedges put on top of the "wall" anchor the top soil through their roots and reduce speed of run-off. Shrubs planted on the face provide deep anchorage.

The two solutions presented in Figure B.14 are aimed at stabilizing less-steep slopes with no imported fill. The solution presented on the left uses wood poles to build a mesh for plant cuttings. The wood trellis has only a medium-term operational life that the shrubs will replace. The solution on the right utilizes plants to complement the effect of the gabions.

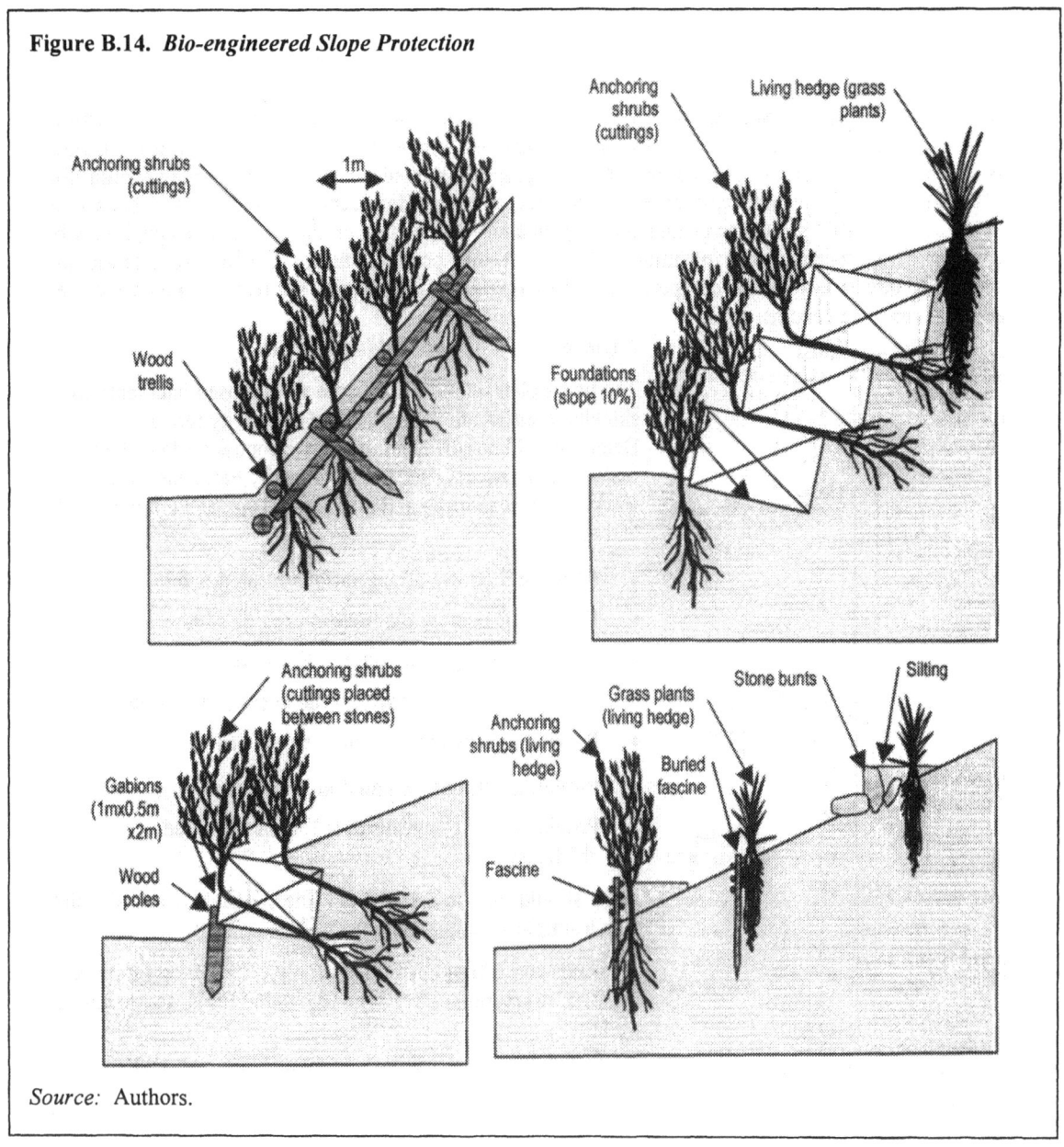

Figure B.14. *Bio-engineered Slope Protection*

Source: Authors.

The solutions above are aimed at controlling erosion on a moderate slope. The diagram on the left demonstrates the use of gabions that are durable. Cuttings are placed between the stones and complement stabilization in the long term. The diagram on the right presents three solutions for moderate slopes. The life of the fascines will be limited and plants are therefore the only long-term solution. Bushes or grasses can be used interchangeably as long as the density is high enough.

Appropriate Engineering Design of RTI

Often, the terms of reference (TOR) used as the basis for RTI designs are adapted from those used for the design of major highways. Such designs require a thorough survey with cross-sections at short intervals and vertical and horizontal alignments. However, such an approach is not justified for RTI if the costs are to remain within reasonable proportion of the planned investment (about 6 percent). The approach for RTI should be simpler and directed towards the production of line diagrams focusing on trouble spots for the solutions of which detailed designs need to be produced. Further details as to the design approach for RTI is discussed in Box B.3.

Box B.3. *Essential Requirements for RTI Engineering Services*

An Initial Road-Condition Survey

This survey should look at the existing level of access and determine the types of interventions necessary to secure the agreed basic access standard. Surveys should include a simple linear access plan indicating surface conditions, gradients, water crossings, and an outline of proposed remedial action. The survey should also include assessments of existing traffic, population densities, and prevailing economic activities. This survey will form the basis for initial project screening and prioritization. Depending on the program design, it may be necessary to carry out participatory planning exercises at this point to assess community interest and competence. This may be beyond the competence of the engineering consultants, but they should be involved in the exercise as resource persons.

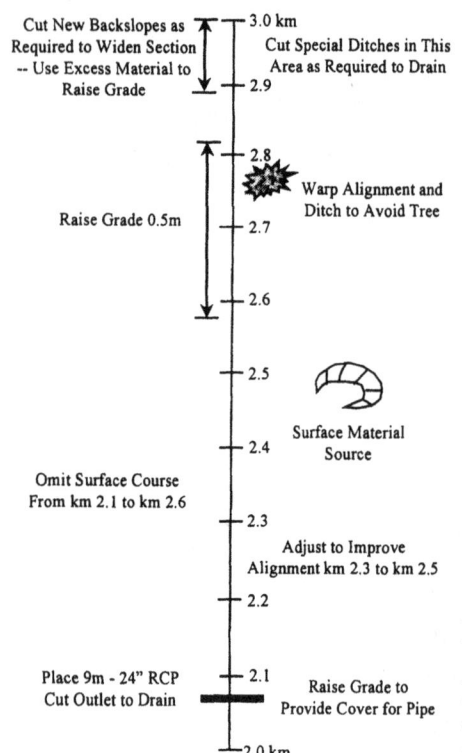

Engineering Design of Spot Improvements

The linear plan should incorporate all proposed interventions, showing their location and the type of activity required. Details should be sufficient to allow a contractor to make a realistic estimate of costs, but is generally based on typical works rather than measured quantities. Typical work items will include:

- Clearing roadway of vegetation to stated width
- Reshaping existing roadway to provide camber
- Raising road grade to the specified level
- Providing side drains with scour checks as indicated
- Providing stone masonry or concrete drift
- Providing turnouts at stated intervals, and
- Providing gravel surface of 0.15cm compacted thickness.

Items should be summarized by linear quantity, and detailed with a simple specification.

Drawings and Bill of Quantities should be provided for more complex structures such as bridges, vented fords, and retaining walls.

Preparation of contract documents

The nature of these documents depend on the contract method adopted. For full competitive bidding where there is an active contracting sector, following the common procedures in the country or region is recommended. If these procedures are considered inappropriate for these types of small-scale works, then the FIDIC Short Form of Contract is recommended as a basis for the development of tailor-made documentation.

If non-competitive community contracting is used, the documents should be designed to ensure that the prices are adequate to cover the labor and material inputs required from the community, and to provide sufficient checks on progress and output.

Supervision and administration of the contract

For the level of works involved in basic access, a full-time consulting engineer as the employer's representative may not be justified. A trained "clerk of works" or the equivalent should ensure day-to-day quality with monthly visits by the engineer to monitor progress and certify payment.

However, if the services of the engineer are to include an element of training and development for the contractors, different arrangements will have to be put in place. This should not be considered as a cost to the road intervention but rather as an element of the overall program development process.

Source: H. Beenhakker et al, 1987, and authors.

Executing the Works

Rural transport infrastructure has traditionally been executed directly by a road agency or local government organization as a force account operation. Evidence in many countries has shown that this approach is ineffective and inefficient and one of the root causes for the poor state of many rural road networks.

The favored approach is to use existing commercial procedures, contracting out the work on a competitive basis wherever possible. However, it has to be recognized that commercialization of the road sector is in its infancy in many developing countries and the private sector is often inexperienced and poorly equipped for road work at the central level. The situation at the local level is generally much worse.

While this makes commercial implementation difficult, basic access interventions have the advantage that they are relatively simple and straightforward, and training local firms and organizations is therefore relatively easier. In addition, the use of labor-based methods ensures that equipment investment costs are low and more within the means of small contractors.

The basic requirements are: to identify potential contractors, including their needs and limitations; introduce appropriate contract procedures; develop training and support packages; and then implement the work in parallel with a capacity-building exercise for the client (in this case the identified owner of the infrastructure), and the local construction industry.

There is now considerable experience in this process and a number of alternative routes that can be followed. The recent ILO publication *Capacity Building for Contracting in the Construction Sector*[100] is primarily aimed at rural roads using labor-based methods and draws on worldwide examples over the past decade.

Contracts are not limited to commercial competitive bidding, but include the use of government contracting agencies, appointed agents that use a development team approach, large-scale contractors that manage small emerging firms as subcontractors, and community contracts with the benefiting communities.

An overview of alternative arrangements is shown in the Table B.2 below.[101] The choice is totally dependent on local experience and resources, but the long-term aim must be to develop procedures and practices that will be sustainable in the local economic and political framework once donor funding ceases. Future maintenance will be largely dependent on the success of this phase.

Table B.2. Alternative Arrangements for Executing Basic Access

Production Arrangement	Contracting					Communities
Approach	Using Established		Developing Small-scale			
Delivery Mechanism	Conventional	Sub-contract	Government-run	Agency	Development Team	Community Groups
Diagram	Employer ↔ Established Contractor ---- Laborers	Employer ↔ Established Contractor ↔ Small Contractor ---- Laborers	Employer ↔ Small Contractor ---- Laborers	Employer ↔ AGETIP / Consulting Firm ◆ Small Contractor ---- Laborers	Employer ↔ Consulting Firm and/or Established Contractor / Small Contractor ---- Laborers	Employer ↔ Community Groups ---- Laborers
Countries (examples)	South Africa, Namibia	India, Nepal, Egypt, South Africa	Benin, Cambodia, Ghana, India, Indonesia, Kenya, Lesotho, Madagascar, Namibia, Nepal, Sierra Leone, South Africa, Tanzania, Uganda, Zambia	AGETIP: Benin, Burkina Faso, Chad, The Gambia, Guinea-Bissau, Madagascar, Namibia, Mali, Mauritania, Niger, Senegal, Tanzania, Consulting Firm: Nepal, South Africa	South Africa	Nepal, Nicaragua, South Africa, Uganda

Legend:
↔ contractual relationships
---- employment relationships
— other relationships

Source: Adapted from Stock and de Veen, 1996.

However, even the definition of small-scale contractor can be very flexible, as illustrated in the following examples from Ghana and Nicaragua.

Box B.4. *Two Examples of Small Contracts*

Department of Feeder Roads, Ghana
More than a decade ago, the Highway Authority in Ghana decided to develop a new class of small contractor contractors. A typical contractor employs up to 200 workers using labor-based techniques, has approximately $150,000 worth of small equipment, and is capable of producing 30 km of engineered gravel road annually. Some 96 contractors have been trained to date. Contracts are awarded under specially adapted FIDIC conditions

Atlantic Coast Transport Program, Nicaragua
The Atlantic Coast Regions of Nicaragua are significantly underdeveloped compared to the rest of the country, with many isolated communities and difficult communications. DANIDA has been involved in a comprehensive program of assisting local municipalities and communities to rehabilitate and improve their transport network. Much of the work has focused on achieving basic access by improving tracks and footpaths.

Engineering design and supervision are the responsibility of the specially established program teams, but the work is carried out mainly by small labor-only community contracts. These contracts typically involve 25 workers who appoint a leader who signs the contract and organizes the group. The leader receives training from program staff.

Rates are decided by program staff based on daily output levels set by the workforces themselves. Since communities are inexperienced in this type of work, program staff should especially ensure that workers are adequately paid and properly equipped.

Source: Authors.

Maintenance of Basic Access Roads

Effective maintenance is the most important prerequisite for safeguarding the investment and ensuring that the road serves its purpose over the anticipated lifetime. A road should not be rehabilitated or constructed if maintenance cannot be afforded and managed. Low-volume roads in tropical and subtropical climates require careful and usually continuous maintenance throughout the year. Part of maintenance management is also effective traffic control to avoid unnecessary damage (excessive loading, traffic during heavy rains). For basic access roads, the following operations are necessary: routine maintenance, grading and periodic maintenance.

Routine Maintenance: Routine maintenance involves drainage opening and repair, carriageway repair, vegetation control, and erosion control on slopes. All of these operations are carried out using labor. All-year routine maintenance, basically on a daily basis, is required for roads in high rainfall areas, while roads that experience low rainfall require less attention during the dry season (Box B.5).

> **Box B.5.** *Labor-Based Routine Maintenance*
>
> Labor-based methods are particularly suitable for routine maintenance of basic access roads. All activities can be carried out using labor only with the exception of grading and compaction, which are only necessary on higher traffic roads. There are basically four different labor-based contract types for routine maintenance:
>
> - **Single-length person contract:** a contract for a defined section of a road (1 to 2 km) is given to an individual
> - **Petty contract (or labor group):** a contract is given to a very small contractor who in turn employs a small team (5 to 10 laborers) to maintain a defined section of a road (5 to 20 km)
> - **Small-scale contract for a particular road:** a contract is given to a small-scale contractor who employs laborers to maintain a particular road or a longer road section (20 to 100 km), and
> - **Small-scale contract for a specified road network:** a contract is given to a small-scale contractor to maintain a specified road network, such as a full maintenance area covering all earth and gravel roads (100 to 300 km of roads).
>
> The **length-person system**, whereby small and manageable tasks are allocated to individual workers (according to priorities throughout the seasons), is the cornerstone of all the approaches, and is therefore explained in more detail below.
>
> **System:**
> A laborer is appointed for each section of road, typically 1 to 2 km in length. A supervisor provides tools and monitors the condition of the road, directs operations, makes reports, and authorizes payments for satisfactory work. This person may be able to supervise up to 10 laborers or 20 km of roads. The laborer lives adjacent to the location of the maintenance activities and therefore does not require any transport. The task rate system is ideal for this sort of work.
>
> The **advantage** of the length-person system is that a continuous maintenance of the entire road can be guaranteed at all times and that one person is responsible for a specific road section. This system is particularly useful in high rainfall areas where, for example, the opening of culverts and mitre drains needs to be carried out on the entire stretch of road almost on a daily basis.
>
> The **disadvantage** is that supervision has to take place on each and every section of the road, which means that each laborer has to be individually instructed. The supervisor therefore must be very mobile and the laborers must be well-trained so that they can work independently. A large part of the time the supervisor is busy traveling from length-person to length-person. The length-person system can easily be transformed into a group system by pulling a number of laborers together and giving them a group task. This is of particular interest to contractors who would like to rationalize their supervision input.
>
> **Transport and Tools:**
> Transport is required for the supervisor (bicycle) and for the contractor (pick-up) to oversee all maintenance work and to transport tools and materials.
>
> Each length-person requires a standard set of hand tools: hoe, shovel, grass-cutter, bush knife, and a rake or spreader.
>
> Two or three length-persons may share: a wheelbarrow (to haul gravel from stockpiles or remove silt and organic material) and an earth rammer (for pothole filling). The gang leader requires a basic set of measuring aids: tape measure, ditch template, spirit level, strings, and pegs. In some projects it may also be necessary to provide the leader with a long-handled shovel and trowel to clean out culverts.
>
> *Source:* Authors.

Grading: Grading is part of the routine maintenance procedure for unpaved roads. It is required to remove ruts and corrugations and generally reestablish the water-shedding qualities of the surface. The operation can require heavy machinery but, fortunately, this is not typically required for the lowest-volume roads. Labor equipped with handtools can achieve adequate results for low-speed basic access. However, where grading is unavoidable due to higher traffic volumes, one to two cycles may be required annually for low-volume roads. This operation can be carried out with a motor grader, but more appropriately with intermediate equipment, like a light tractor-towed grader (Box B.6).

Box B.6. *Grading of Basic Access Roads*

For basic access road maintenance, mechanized grading is in most cases not necessary. Experience from various projects has shown that the carriageway of these roads can be maintained by labor alone. However, for roads with a traffic level close to 50 VPD and with a surface material that is relatively weak, grading is an option. For maintenance grading, intermediate equipment (tractor-towed graders) can achieve the desired results, and for lighter operations, a tire drag is often sufficient. For maintenance purposes, there are two types of grading operations:

Heavy grading:
- used when the surface has a severe amount of potholes and ruts. Done preferably at the beginning of the rainy season, and/or at the end of the wet season when the moisture content of the surfacing material is still enough to help re-compaction;
- scarifying and cutting to the bottom of the deformation;
- reshaping the surface;
- compacting loose material.

Light grading:
- used when the surface is corrugated and rough;
- light trimming of the surface;
- light compaction of the loose material would be advantageous, preferably during the wet season or when the surface material still has some moisture content to allow for compaction.

Surface material with a relatively high clay content can be more easily graded when still moist. Best practice experience suggests that grading frequency for roads with a traffic level of 50 VPD is two times per year, of which one grading should be heavy and one grading would be light. The costs for maintenance grading are in the range of $250 to 400 per km and cycle.

Source: Authors.

Periodic Maintenance: Periodic maintenance for gravel roads involves replacing the gravel-wearing course. This is also termed regravelling. Depending on the traffic level and the climate, a regravelling cycle of five to eight years is common (Box B.7). Usually not only does the gravel surface have to be renewed, but reshaping work of the formation, reinstatement of the drainage, and other repair work are required at the same time.

Box B.7. *Gravel Loss*

Good surface maintenance is a prerequisite to safeguarding the gravel layer and to reducing maintenance expenditures. Maintenance engineers need to carefully assess the gravel surface condition on at least a yearly basis and monitor the gravel loss. The loss is never uniform along the entire road and partial regravelling is often the most cost-effective approach.

The rate of the gravel loss is mainly determined by the traffic, the gravel quality, and the prevailing climate. For example, with an average daily traffic of less than 50 VPD, the loss of lateritic gravel is in the range of 10 to 30 mm depending on the annual rainfall (1000 mm to 3000 mm, respectively).

As rule of thumb, a gravel layer needs to be replaced every five to eight years.

Source: Authors.

Regravelling is the most expensive maintenance operation for unpaved roads and over the lifetime of a road may cost the same, or even more than initial construction. The reality in most developing countries is that regravelling is rarely or never done when necessary. This is not entirely due to bad management and lack of funds. In some countries, suitable gravel is reported to be a rapidly diminishing resource. The result is that roads deteriorate until they are no longer maintainable and have to be reconstructed long before their planned design life expires.

Most basic access roads will not be fully gravelled. However, all those sections that are gravelled will still be subject to a wearing process and will need renewal at some stage. Rather than setting up a periodic program that may not be affordable by local government or the communities, an alternative is to integrate regravelling operations into routine maintenance. Spot regravelling can then be carried out annually as required. Gravel is stockpiled at key points and the entire operation can then be carried out labor-intensively by the routine maintenance contractors.

The Costs of Alternative RTI Road Improvements

Exact figures for the construction and maintenance costs of basic access roads cannot be provided (as prevailing conditions and input costs differ from country to country, and project to project). There can also be significant differences in the logistics of a project, especially the costs for hauling material, the availability of suitable tools and equipment, and the skills and experience of supervisors and workers. However, some guidance from best practice projects is useful for providing likely ranges. Box B.8 gives a general indication of the likely range of costs for spot improvement, construction, and maintenance of basic access roads in different circumstances. Before any conclusions can be drawn in a particular circumstance, detailed cost analysis of the possible alternatives should be carried out. Such analysis should always investigate total life-cycle-cost (construction and maintenance).

Box B.8. *Estimated Costs for Spot Improvement, New Construction, and Maintenance of Basic Access Roads (all single-lane roads)*

Spot improvement to existing motorable track
In rolling and flat terrain and low rainfall	$1,500 to 2,500/km
In mountainous and high-rainfall area	$5,000 to 20,000/km

Construction
Earth-road construction in mountainous areas	$10,000 to 50,000/km
Earth-road construction in hilly and flat areas, no embankment required	$6,000 to 15,000/km
Earth-road construction in flat areas, embankment required	$8,000 to 30,000/km
Gravel surface, 12 to 15 cm compacted, 3.5 to 4.5 m wide, hauling distance between 2 and 8 km	$5,000 to 8,000/km
Stone pavement, 20 to 30 cm strong, sealed, three to four m wide	$10,000 to 15,000/km
Surface dressing, (single seal, double seal)	$2 to 3 per square meter
Clay or concrete brick paving (or 5cm asphalt concrete layer)	$8 to 10 per square meter

Maintenance
Routine maintenance of gravel road (by labor)	$200 to 600 km/year
Grading of gravel road (by equipment: average of light and heavy)	$250 to 400 km/cycle
Periodic maintenance (regravelling every five to eight years)	$5,000 to 8,000/km

Note: Construction costs include all construction work (contracted out) plus design and contract supervision, but do not include agency costs. The costs include an average number of small structures (for example, drifts, multiple culverts) and water crossings (splashes, small drifts, or culverts), but not bridges.

Source: Authors.

APPENDIX C
DESIGNING BASIC ACCESS RTI FOR NON-MOTORIZED MEANS OF TRANSPORT

Introduction

For local short-distance movements and non-motorized transport users, simple improvements to paths and tracks can be of significant benefit to local communities by making them safer and easier to use. In addition, strategic investments can often reduce seasonal or sporadic periods of poor passability. In general, improvements of water crossings are the most cost-effective and easy-to-identify problem spots, although, in some cases, surface improvements (such as gravelling and stone pitching) of high-traffic sections might also be merited. The most common problems on paths and trails that reduce functionality are:

- slipperiness and erosion (caused by poor drainage or steep gradients),
- wet, marshy, or seasonally flooded areas of poor passability,
- dangerously steep and/or rocky sections, and
- difficult and/or seasonal stream or river crossings.

Identifying Problems on Paths and Tracks

Identifying access constraints on paths and tracks begins with consultation with users and a visual field survey to identify local conditions (soils, drainage, and grade). Local users identify the most heavily traveled and problematic routes in and around villages and to major destination points, as well as what type of transport takes place over those routes. They make distinctions between regular and seasonal problems. A rapid field survey is required to get a picture of local conditions and help in selecting preliminary strategies for overcoming current problems. If necessary, a further technical survey may be undertaken after initial consultations to obtain more precise observations and measurements of the paths and tracks identified. An outline of a technical survey is given in Box C.1.

Box C.1. *Technical Survey of Path or Track*

Technical surveys are carried out to gather information on the physical condition of a path or track. Information is usually only recorded for the section where there are existing or potential problems. The type of observations and measurements required are:

- reference number and location of section (relative to obvious landmarks),
- length of section (can be paced, but preferably measured with a tape),
- soil type,
- gradient of path or trail,
- crossfall (sideways slope) of surrounding land,
- type of problem (slippery section, erosion), and
- details of the situation with possible solutions (sketches and notes).

The survey is usually carried out by an engineer or technician, but it is preferable if the technician is accompanied by the users of the path or track, who can point out or confirm the problem areas.

Source: Gary Taylor, 1994.

Design of Improvements

As is the case with motorized access, the design of path and track improvements requires knowledge concerning local conditions (terrain, soils, and environment), local institutional capacity and arrangements, transport patterns and other problems. After initial technical information concerning problems (and possible solutions) has been collected, the next step is to obtain information concerning the level and types of traffic. For high-volume paths and tracks, this may require traffic counts, while for very low-volume situations, estimates based on population served may yield sufficient accuracy. For engineering requirements, the primary concern of the transport survey is to assess design options based on users (types and sizes of loads and vehicles) and the level of daily traffic along the path or tracks. The information that should be collected includes daily and hourly counts of the numbers and types of means of transport and porters and their loading characteristics. If there is a need to prioritize among alternative investments, these counts can be supplemented with on-site user surveys to collect the information for priority evaluation. The survey process described in Appendix D can be adapted to paths and tracks.

Typical Improvements

Once traffic and loading characteristics have been determined, standard design parameters are used to determine the appropriate level of investment. Most often, the least-cost method for improving paths and trails to all-weather passability is community-driven spot improvements. In some cases, where transport demand is high and benefits adequate, full upgrading of the path or track along its entire length may be justified. Technical assistance is needed for designing the spot improvements and managing the works.

Essential first-stage design parameters for basic access paths or trails are camber and crossfall, width, and gradient:

- *Camber and Crossfall*—Camber and crossfall are essential for proper surface drainage and should be a minimum of 5 percent in rainy areas, and higher in areas of heavy seasonal rain. A camber as low as 3 percent is possible in arid areas, but flat paths and tracks are not recommended.

- *Width*—Width is determined by the requirements for passing and the loading characteristics (dimensions) of the NMT using the path. For basic access footpaths, one-way pedestrian traffic requires a width of approximately one meter. For tracks, animal or cart-loading characteristics will determine the required width and should be considered. A typical single-lane track will have a width of 1.4 meters.

- *Maximum Gradient*—Paths are common in hilly or mountainous areas where road construction is difficult or too costly. The maximum gradient depends on the composition of the traffic. Pedestrians can ascend very steep slopes, although steps are necessary above 26 percent. However, wheeled vehicles and heavily loaded porters require much shallower gradients. The desirable maximum longitudinal gradients together with a summary of basic access standards for non-motorized access are summarized in Table C.1.

Table C.1. *Basic Standards for Non-Motorized Access*			
Feature	Terrain		
	Flat	Rolling	Steep
Path width	1 to 2 m, depending on traffic density and type	1 to 2 m, depending on traffic density and type	1 m
Path surface	In-situ soils except on sand or steep erodible slopes		
Camber	5%	5%	5%
Maximum gradient	N/A	7% for bicycles 8% for animal drawn carts 12% for pedestrians and pack animals 26 to 70% for pedestrians when steps provided	
Drainage structures and water crossings	Stepping stones, timber footbridges, suspension bridges		
Special features	Earth or brushwood causeways in marshy areas	Timber water bars	Hairpin bends, steps, handrails, timber water bars
Source: Authors.			

Surfacing

Most paths and tracks have developed naturally from the passage of traffic. The compaction of the soil by pedestrians, animals, and light vehicles is usually sufficient to give a satisfactory surface. The addition or replacement of surfacing material is relatively expensive and can only be justified in special circumstances such as the occurrence of marshy areas, very rough terrain, very sandy soils, or easily erodible soils on steep slopes.

Where the major problem is an erodible surface, a single layer of well compacted gravelly soil may be adequate. A certain amount of clay mixed in with the gravel helps bind the material to produce a dense impermeable surface layer. Stone pitching or "Telford" construction may be necessary for heavy traffic or on steep gradients. Figure C.1 illustrates some of these methods.

In wet or marshy areas, it is necessary to use different techniques to minimize the costs. There are three main approaches:[102]

- Stepping stones or stone causeways, in which large stones are firmly set in the ground to provide a stable walkway. This is only suitable for pedestrian traffic.

- Rafts or boardwalks, in which a timber walkway is built to sit on top of the wet soil. These are usually of light construction, for pedestrian or cycle traffic only.

- Turnpike sections, where the path or track is raised as a small embankment, with the edge constrained by logs or rocks. Brushwood or geo-textile membranes may be used to prevent the embankment from sinking. This is a relatively expensive solution suitable for short stretches of 50 meters or less. This approach is also useful for areas of loose sand.

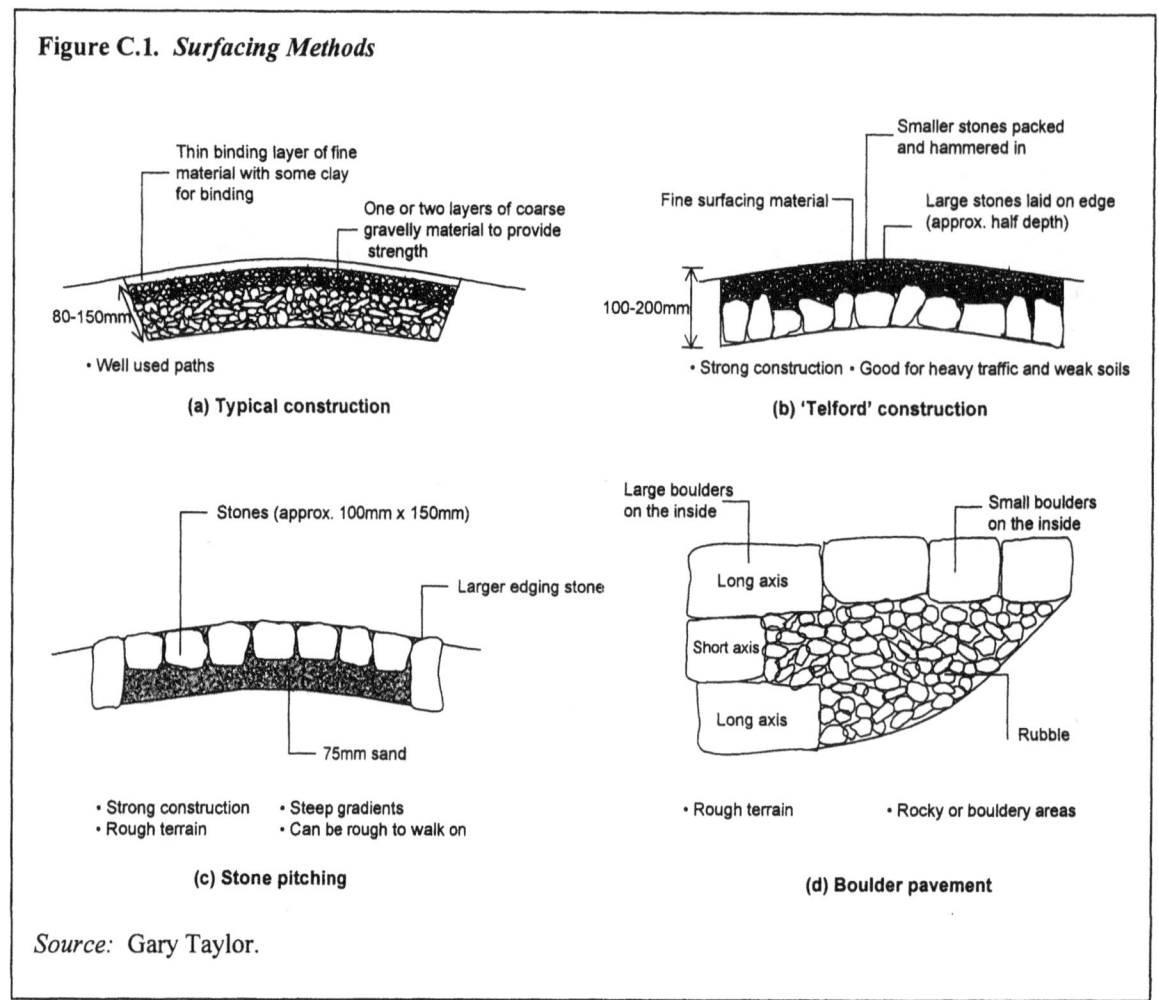

Figure C.1. *Surfacing Methods*

Source: Gary Taylor.

Erosion Control

Surface water running down paths and tracks must be diverted before it erodes or saturates the surface. Similarly, surface water in ditches must also be diverted from those ditches before the bottoms begin to erode. Areas of natural water cross-flow must be managed in order to properly maintain surface and formation integrity. The primary low-cost methods of diverting water from non-motorized road surfaces are water-bars and drifts.

Design guidelines for the use of water-bars are given in Figure C.2.

For very steep gradients where only foot traffic is anticipated, it may be appropriate to build steps. However, these must be properly dimensioned to allow people carrying heavy loads to keep up a constant rhythm when ascending or descending. Tread lengths should be between one-half and one meter (equivalent to one or two paces) and the rise should be in the order of 160 to 250 mm. In any flight of steps, the rise should be consistent throughout.

Figure C.2. *Water-Bar Guidelines*

Gradient of path	Angle of water-bar
5%	$25°$
10%	$35°$
12%	$45°$

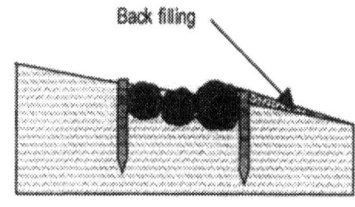

Recommended spacing of water-bars (meters)

	Longitudinal Gradient in %					
Type of soil	2	4	6	8	10	12
Loam	100	50	30	20	15	*
Clay-sand	150	100	60	50	30	15
Clay or clay-gravel	-	150	90	60	50	30
Gravel/rocky	-	-	230	150	100	80

* Gradient not recommended in this type of soil

- Water-bar not usually required

Source: Authors.

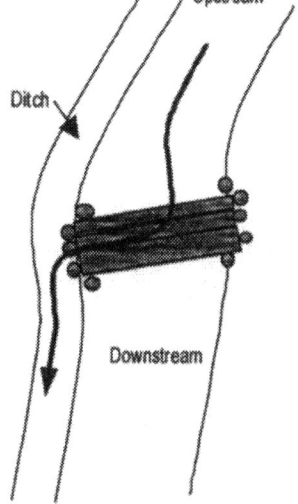

Timber, Culverts, and Footbridges

It is not usually necessary or cost-effective to use concrete culverts or other substantial structures for non-motorized access. However, timber culverts and footbridges can be used for continuous or deep stream and river crossings.

These structures do not have the strength of normal highway structures, and it is important that access is restricted to avoid overloading. Ensuring that the structures are less than two-meters wide is the most reliable approach.

Examples of a timber culvert, and design parameters for a timber footbridge are given in Table C.2 and Figure C.3 below. For long spans over deep water or gorges, the best approach is the construction of a suspension bridge. This is a specialized structure that should be designed by an experienced engineer. A number of publications are available covering this area.[103]

The following table relates the maximum clear span to the diameter of the logs required.

Table C.2. *Timber Footbridge*

Maximum clear span (meters)	3	6	9	12	15
Log diameter (centimeters)	20	25	30	40	50

Source: Authors.

Figure C.3. *Timber Culvert*

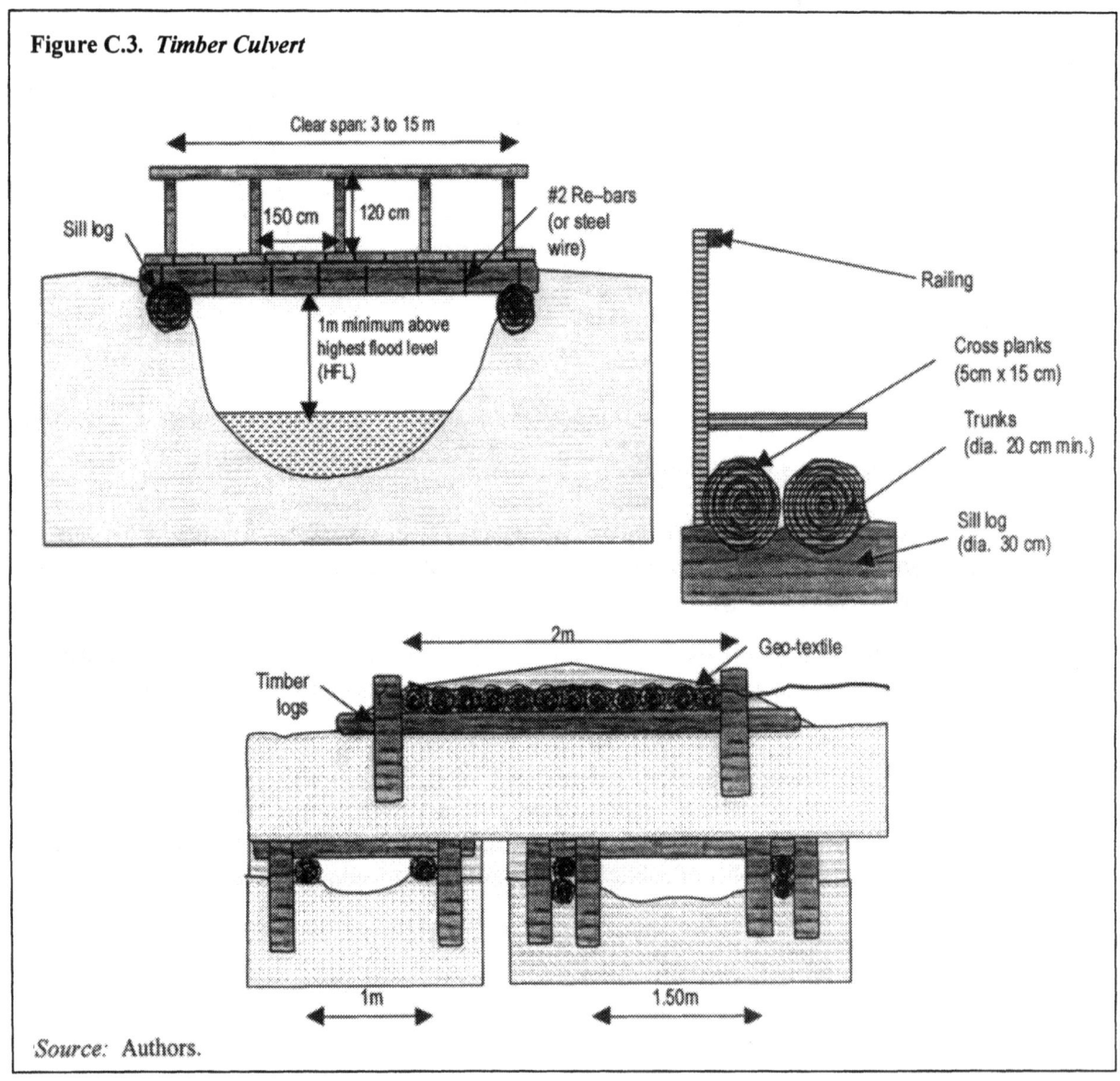

Source: Authors.

APPENDIX D
LOW-COST TRAFFIC SURVEY METHODS FOR RTI

Rural transport planners often face a lack of traffic data concerning RTI, and scarce resources for collecting new data. In addition, there may be weak institutional capacity for data collection and management at the local government or community level, which can be further compounded by poorly defined networks, ownership, and responsibilities.

Information on traffic, however, is essential for effective design and appraisal of RTI, particularly when upgrading to a higher than least-cost basic access standard or for investments motivated by economic objectives. If proposed improvements are to be appraised on a cost-effectiveness basis, traffic data samples should be collected and correlated with other indicators, such as populations served by the particular RTI. For socioeconomic impact studies, household-level mobility studies are required, including data on means of transport, trip purpose, origin and destination of trip and duration, in addition to other socioeconomic data.

The following two types of low-cost traffic surveys are described here:

- Moving Observer Count (MOC)
- Manual Traffic Survey (MTS)

The MOC is a rapid method of assessment suitable for categorizing roads into broad flow bands. The MTS is a more discerning and complete survey method, but requires considerable capacity and resources for appropriate execution.

Traffic Survey Form and Calculation of Average Daily Traffic (ADT)

A sample of a typical survey form is attached to this appendix. It can be used for both MOC and MTS surveys. Different categories of motorized and non-motorized vehicles are listed. These can be adjusted to reflect the actual existing types of vehicles in use in a particular area. "Weights" for the different means of transport are sometimes used for converting different vehicle types to Passenger Car Units (PCU).[104] Manual traffic counts normally should last 12 daylight hours. To get daily (24 hours) traffic, the 12-hours traffic would then normally have to be multiplied by a factor of 1.33. The Average Daily Traffic (ADT) would be calculated as the average of the seven days' count of the total daily "weighted" traffic.

Moving Observer Count (MOC)

MOC can be carried out by the evaluation team or by an inspector from the local government rural roads agency. The survey can be executed at any location of a particular road section but should last at least one hour. Utilizing the form proposed in this appendix, the different types of vehicles need to be put into three different categories: (a) vehicles traveling in the opposite direction (x); (b) vehicles overtaking observer (y); and (c) vehicles overtaken by the observer (z). Following will then be the hourly traffic in both directions (HT):

$$HT = (x + y - z) / t$$

(t = period of survey measured in hours). To convert the hourly flow into daily flows the following formula normally applies:

$$DT = 16 \times HT$$

Manual Traffic Survey (MTS)

Manual traffic counts, using an adaptation of the form introduced in (1) above, should be used on all RTI network sections which are earmarked for upgrading to higher than basic access standard (including the upgrading from non-motorized basic access to motorized basic access). As mentioned in (2) above, a seven-day, 12-hour count is recommended. In particular circumstances, for example, in hotter climates where night travel is common, 24-hour counts might be warranted. It is important that both motorized and non-motorized traffic is counted and, in the case of non-motorized access only, obviously, human porterage must be counted as well. Seasonal variations might be important, and, if possible, counts should be conducted during various seasons of high- and low-traffic flows. Counts should be done far enough away from urban or village areas, so results are not distorted by local traffic activities.

Origin-destination (OD)-surveys, including trip purpose and duration of trips might be warranted in certain circumstances, especially if new RTI and major new alignments are planned. If overloaded trucks are prevalent, an axle-load survey might be required.

Rural roads agencies should carry out traffic surveys on all major sections of their network on a regular basis (at least annually). With experience, certain patterns will be established and time and efforts for individual surveys will be reduced. Such patterns include: typical seasonal variations, traffic composition, the share of night-time to day-time traffic, growth factors, and the correlation between traffic and villages size.

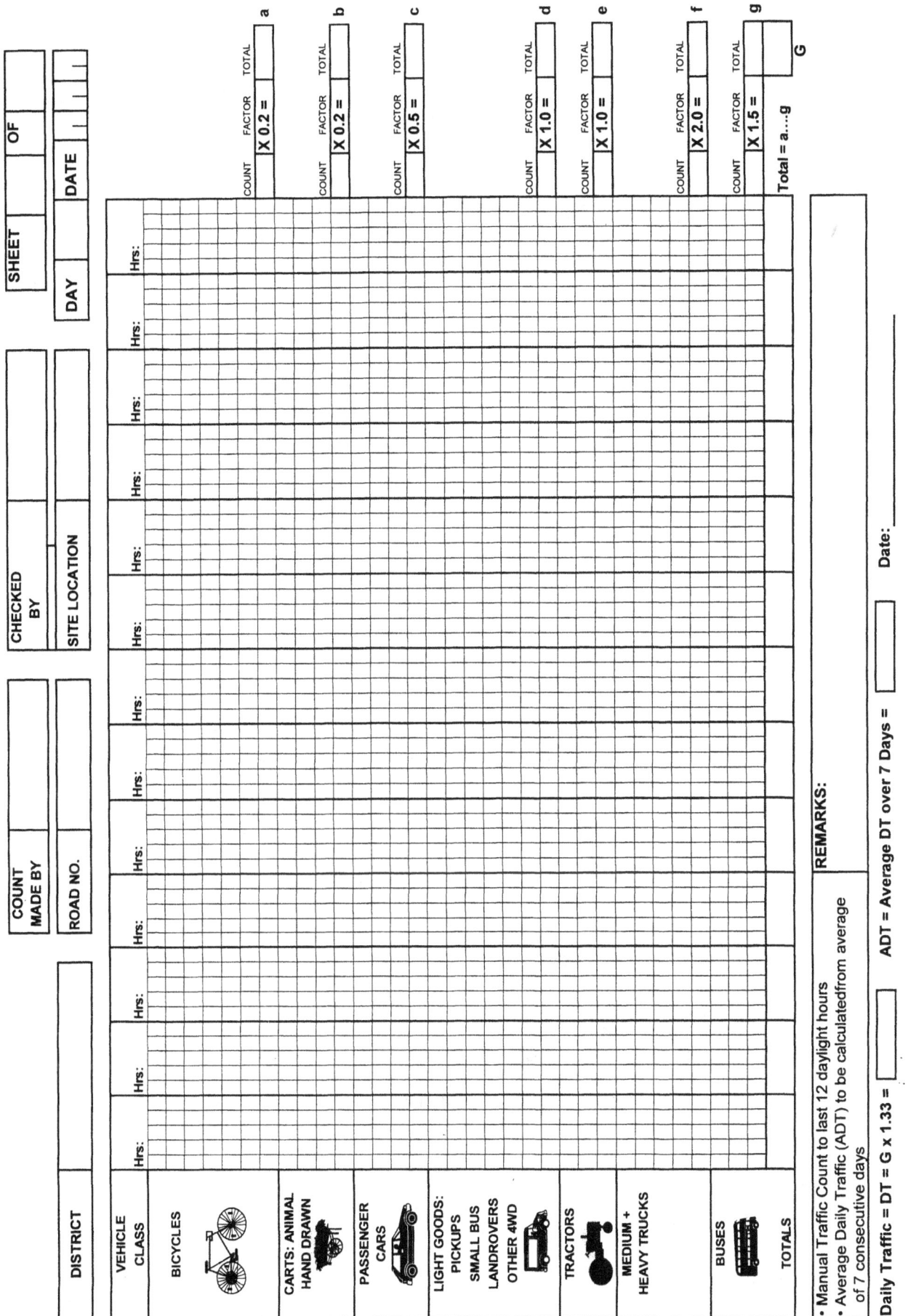

APPENDIX E
SAMPLES OF INNOVATIVE ECONOMIC APPRAISALS OF RTI INVESTMENTS

Appendix E.1
India - Andhra Pradesh
Rural Roads Component of Economic Restructuring Project
(Based on World Bank Infrastructure Note RT-5, January 2000, prepared by Liu Zhi)

Introduction

Rural road projects that aim to improve basic road accessibility from villages to markets and social services are expected to yield not only savings in vehicle operating cost (VOC) and road-user travel time cost (TTC), but also substantial social values in the form of broadened socioeconomic opportunities for the rural population. As most rural access roads have very low-traffic volumes, the social values generated from the improvement of basic access are often a more important item of project benefits than the direct road-user cost savings. Due to the difficulties in quantifying the social values in monetary terms, the road cost-benefit analysis methodology that quantifies road-user benefits mainly as VOC and TTC savings is unsuitable for evaluating rural basic access road projects. Alternative methodologies should be adopted. This appendix describes an application of cost-effectiveness analysis (CEA) to supplement cost-benefit analysis (CBA) in the evaluation and selection of road works for financing under a Bank rural road project in the state of Andhra Pradesh, India. An overview of the project is provided in a separate World Bank Infrastructure Note (Transport No. RT-4, January 2000).

An Overview of the Economic Analysis

The project area includes three selected poor rural districts, Adilabad, Karimnagar, and Warangal, with a total population of 6.8 million. The project is proposed to improve the rural road network to at least basic, all-weather passable standard. The rural road network totals 15,000 km, most of which is in poor condition. Almost 60 percent of the network are tracks and earth roads, 10 percent gravel, and 30 percent water-bound macadam (WBM) roads. Neither tracks nor earth roads are all-weather passable. Both gravel and WBM roads can be all-weather passable, but many of them do not meet the all-weather standard due to broken or missing cross-drainage facilities. The role of economic analysis is to assist the design, prioritization, and selection of road works for financing under the project.

The demand for network investment greatly exceeds the project budget. The key to maximizing investment is focusing on the improvement of a core network that would ensure minimum connectivity for *each* village to a nearby main road or market center. The core network is identified through a rural road master planning process.[105] Its links that do not meet the basic all-weather standard are identified as candidate roads for improvement, and economic analysis is only applied to these roads.

Road works for candidate roads fall into two major categories: (a) *basic accessibility works*, including upgrading tracks and earth roads to gravel or WBM roads, and all minor and major cross drainage works on existing gravel and WBM roads; and (b) *black-topping works* on existing earth, gravel, and WBM roads. Since basic accessibility works are considered as a valuable instrument for poverty reduction, they are given first priority. Black-topping, on the other hand, is carried out primarily for economic reasons. When traffic volume (especially motor vehicle traffic) on an unpaved road reaches a certain level, it is more economical to pave the road rather than to keep restoring the unpaved road to all-weather condition. Economic justification is required for all black-topping works.

Both CBA and CEA methodologies are being used for this project. CBA is applied mainly to the black-topping works. A simple spreadsheet CBA program (shown in an attachment to this appendix), based on the conventional road CBA methodology, is first used to determine minimum traffic thresholds. These thresholds are defined as the combination of motor vehicle (MV) and non-motorized vehicle (NMV) traffic levels at which black-topping would be justified at the minimum economic rate of return (ERR) of 12 percent. They are shown as MV/NMV combinations along the curve in Figure E.1.1. All candidate roads with traffic levels around and above the thresholds are evaluated individually using the spreadsheet CBA program, and the ERRs are estimated. The candidate roads with traffic levels significantly below the thresholds are dropped from the list of black-topping works, but are considered for upgrading to basic access standard and evaluated in the category of basic accessibility works.

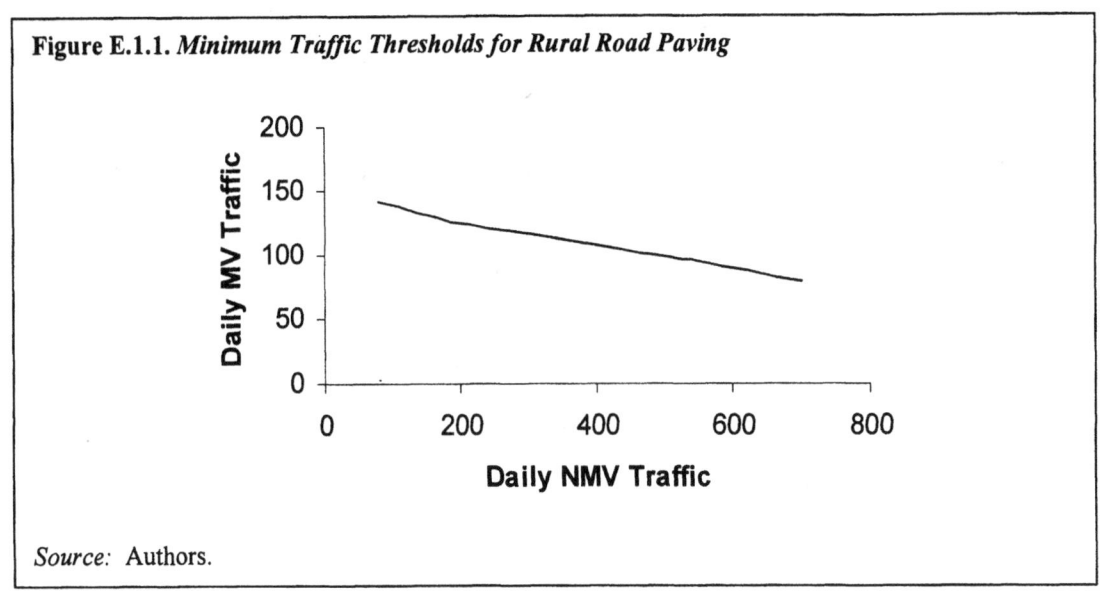

Figure E.1.1. *Minimum Traffic Thresholds for Rural Road Paving*

Source: Authors.

CEA is applied to the selection of basic accessibility road works. All roads proposed for basic accessibility work are ranked by a simple cost-effectiveness measure—total population provided with basic access per $2,500 equivalent of expenditure. The top-ranking least-cost works are then financed, with a maximum of $50 equivalent per person served used as a final restrictive measure to ensure cost-effectiveness.

The economic analysis produces a list of basic accessibility road works ranked by cost-effectiveness and a list of black-topping works ranked by ERR. It should be noted that the application of CBA and CEA in this project does not deal with the optimal budget allocation between the two categories of road works. The allocation is decided through a stakeholder participatory process. Based on the budget allocation about 1,700 km of rural roads are selected for financing to basic accessibility standard, with a cost-effectiveness ratio ranging from $14 to $50 outlay per person served. A further total of 1,300 km of roads are selected for black-topping. Their ERRs range from 12 to 90 percent with an overall ERR of 24 percent. A total of 2 million people are expected to benefit from the project.

Village and Household Transport Survey

The application of CEA for basic accessibility works is supported by an assessment of the likely impact of basic road access on the welfare of rural households. Data was obtained through a small-scale rural household and village transport survey conducted for 40 sampled villages in the project area. For each sampled village, 10 households were randomly selected for the household level survey.

The survey results are summarized in Table E.1.1. below, which reveals significant differences in selected socioeconomic indicators between villages connected with all-weather access road and those unconnected. According to household interviews in the unconnected villages, poor road conditions, seasonal road closures, lack of motorized access, and the high cost of freight delivery are among the major obstacles to village accessibility. Moreover, road closure during the rainy season causes produce spoilage, delay of freight delivery, labor unemployment, and lower school attendance. When asked what impacts are expected from the improvement of roads, most households in both connected and unconnected villages responded with predictions of more seasonal work taken outside villages, higher intensity of cultivation, and expansion of cultivated land. The survey results provided strong empirical evidence to support the social and economic justifications for the provision of basic all-weather access to these villages.

Table E.1.1. *A Summary of Rural Household Survey Results: Villages Connected with All-Weather Access Road versus Villages Unconnected, 1997*

Indicators	Connected	Unconnected
Household income ($/yr.)	700	275
Literacy rate		
Male	51%	40%
Female	35%	22%
Total	43%	32%
Avg. distance traveled for (km)		
Fertilizer	11	19
Seeds	11	19
Pesticides	9	16
Transport cost ($/ton-km)		
Fertilizer by bullock cart	0.13	0.33
Seeds by bullock carts	0.10	0.26
Fertilizer by lorry	0.16	0.25
Seeds by lorry	0.08	0.11
Avg. distance to school		
Primary education	0.2	0.2
Secondary education	2.5	18.0

Source: Authors.

The Spreadsheet CBA Program

The spreadsheet CBA program, shown in Table E.1.3, is designed specifically for the evaluation of rural road black-topping works. It has a conceptual structure similar to that of the HDM model, but is much simplified for rural road evaluation. The program consists of five panels. The first is used to record the road data and economic input parameters. The value of travel time is estimated using the rural per capita income data from the project area. The annual traffic growth rate is predicted based on the area's population and per capita income trends. The second panel contains engineering unit cost data obtained from the field. The third panel presents the estimated unit VOCs and travel speeds by both road type and vehicle type. The average road surface condition for each type of road in the project area is measured by a range of international roughness index (IRI).[106] The unit VOC data for motor vehicles are obtained from the empirical VOC-IRI relationships estimated for a Bank-financed state highway project in Andhra Pradesh, and extended to cover the worst IRI levels typically found on the rural road network. Average travel speed on each type of road surface is estimated by local engineers based on their field experience. The VOC-IRI relationships for bullock carts and bicycles are estimated using the NMV basic cost data (Table 2) collected from the field and the empirical relationships developed by recent studies in South Asia.[107] The fourth panel calculates savings in VOC and value of travel time (VOT) for the users of each mode of transport. Finally, the bottom panel calculates the economic cost and benefit streams over the project life, the net present value (NPV), and the ERR.

Table E.1.2. *NMV Basic Cost Data, 1997*

Item	Unit	Bullock Cart	Bicycle
Vehicle price	US$	62.5	30.0
Price of a pair of ox	US$	312.5	n.a.
Annual cost of feeding the ox	US$/pair	150.0	n.a.
Annualized maintenance cost	US$	75.0	5.0
Vehicle depreciation	US$/yr.	12.5	5.0 (a)
Annual average usage	Km	2,400	1,000
Average year of life	Years	5	10
Average VOC per km	US$	**0.13**	**0.01**

Note: (a) Annual depreciation for the first three years
Source: Authors.

Lessons Learned

1. Where the provision of basic road access is mainly for social equity reasons, cost-effectiveness analysis can be used to evaluate or highlight the impact of the project, and economic efficiency can be considered implicitly through an emphasis on the least-cost design to achieve the project objectives.

2. The economic analysis described here requires systematic data collection. This particular experience may not be transferable to other rural road projects. However, one important lesson learned from this experience is that data collection at low cost can be possible with the active participation of the client in the preparation of the project.

3. Where systematic data do not exist or are costly to collect, effort should be made to at least establish a transport/poverty profile through a small-scale household survey, and to collect traffic data on the proposed rural roads.

4. While the methods used in this project help ensure the application of economic criteria, they do not deal with the optimal allocation of budget between the two categories of road works. This allocation should be decided through a participatory process.

Table E.1.3. *Cost-Benefit Analysis Program for Rural Road Paving Project*

District name:	Warangal	Road name:	PWD to Chilpoor
Division name:	Warangal	Road No.:	L101
Road length (km):	15	Population served:	12,000
Current road type (enter 0 for earth, 1 for gravel, 2 for WBM)	2	No. of minor CD/km:	0.5
		Major CD (m/km):	1.0
Value of travel time (US$/hr)	0.06	Annual traffic growth rate	5%
Annual per capital income growth	3%	Standard Conversion Factor	0.90

	Capital Cost ('000 US$/km)			Annualized Maint Cost ('000 US$/km)	
	Financial	Economic		Financial	Economic
Formation	5.00	4.50	Earth	0.55	0.50
Gravel (when available on site)	5.00	4.50	Gravel	0.68	0.61
WBM (each layer)	6.25	5.63	WBM	0.88	0.79
Blacktop	7.50	6.75	Blacktop	0.93	0.83
Minor CD ('000 US$/each)	5.00	4.50			
Major CD ('000 US$/m)	3.75	3.38			

	Unit VOC by Road Type (US$/km)				Travel Speed by Road Type (Min./km)			
	Earth	Gravel	WBM	BT	Earth	Gravel	WBM	BT
Vehicle Type	IRI=14-18	IRI=9-11	IRI=9-11	IRI=5-7	IRI=14-18	IRI=9-11	IRI=9-11	IRI=5-7
Buses	0.303	0.250	0.245	0.225	2.4	1.7	1.7	1.2
Mini buses	0.170	0.123	0.118	0.100	2.4	1.7	1.7	1.2
Cars/Jeeps	0.170	0.123	0.118	0.100	2.4	1.7	1.7	1.2
Trucks	0.343	0.280	0.268	0.240	2.4	1.7	1.7	1.2
Tractor Trailors	0.250	0.225	0.200	0.150	3.0	2.0	2.0	1.5
LCV/Tempo	0.170	0.123	0.118	0.100	2.4	1.7	1.7	1.2
Three wheelers	0.075	0.063	0.050	0.038	2.4	1.7	1.7	1.2
Two wheelers	0.063	0.038	0.038	0.025	2.4	1.7	1.7	1.2
Bullock carts	0.147	0.129	0.118	0.115	20.0	15.0	15.0	15.0
Bicycles	0.010	0.008	0.008	0.006	7.5	7.0	7.0	6.5
Pedestrains	n.a.	n.a.	n.a.	n.a.	17.0	16.0	16.0	15.5

	Base yr.	Avg. Veh.	VOC(US$/km)		Speed (Min./km)		Savings (US$/km)	
Vehicle Type	Traffic	Occup.	w/o. Proj.	w. Proj.	w/o. Proj	w. Proj.	VOC	VOT
Buses	20	35	0.25	0.23	1.70	1.20	0.40	0.36
Mini buses	16	10	0.12	0.10	1.70	1.20	0.28	0.08
Cars/Jeeps	40	4	0.12	0.10	1.70	1.20	0.70	0.08
Trucks	24	0	0.27	0.24	1.70	1.20	0.66	0.00
Tractor Trailors	22	5	0.20	0.15	2.00	1.50	1.10	0.06
LCV/Tempo	37	1	0.12	0.10	1.70	1.20	0.65	0.02
Three wheelers	32	3	0.05	0.04	1.70	1.20	0.40	0.05
Two wheelers	68	1.5	0.04	0.03	1.70	1.20	0.85	0.05
Bullock carts	60	1.5	0.12	0.12	15.00	15.00	0.15	0.00
Bicycles	320	1	0.01	0.01	7.00	6.50	0.56	0.17
Pedestrians	680	1	n.a.	n.a.	16.00	15.50	n.a.	0.35
MVs (2 2w = 1 MV)	225		Annual sum (325 days/year) =				1868	400
NMVs	380							

				(All in thousand US$)		
Year	Traffic Growth	Capital Cost	Maint. Cost	VOC Savings	VOT Savings	Net Benefit
1998	5%	20.25	0.045	1.87	0.40	-18.03
1999	5%		0.045	1.96	0.43	2.35
2000	5%		0.045	2.06	0.47	2.48
2001	5%		0.045	2.16	0.51	2.62
2002	5%		0.045	2.27	0.55	2.77
2003	5%		0.045	2.38	0.59	2.93
2004	5%		0.045	2.50	0.64	3.10
2005	5%		0.045	2.63	0.69	3.28
2006	5%	6.75	0.045	2.76	0.75	-3.29
2007	5%		0.045	2.90	0.81	3.66
2008	5%		0.045	3.04	0.88	3.87
2009	5%		0.045	3.19	0.95	4.10
2010	5%		0.045	3.35	1.03	4.33
2011	5%		0.045	3.52	1.11	4.59
2012	5%		0.045	3.70	1.20	4.85
2013	5%		0.045	3.88	1.30	5.13
NPV						0.81
ERR						12.8%

Source: Authors.

Appendix E.2
Bhutan Rural Access Project: Economic Analysis[108]

Introduction

An IDA Credit for a "'Rural Access Project' in the Kingdom of Bhutan was approved by the IDA Board in December 1999. The main project objective is to improve access of rural communities to markets, schools, health centers and other economic and social infrastructure, in order to improve the quality of life and productivity of rural communities. The project will, among other things, help construct about 120 kilometers of rural access roads in four districts (dzongkhag) in Bhutan, where people have to walk an average of two days to reach the nearest road. Bhutan has good agricultural potential, but its villages are on the slopes of the Himalayan range, and a lack of access roads is a major socioeconomic problem. The Royal Government of Bhutan (RGOB) attaches great importance to improving rural access, as it will provide rural communities better access to markets, schools and health centers, and also help prevent rural-to-urban migration.

The note presented below is essentially Annex 4 of the Project Appraisal Document (PAD; IDA report no.19795-BHU, dated November 19, 1999). It summarizes the economic analysis of one project road, the Dakpai-Buli road (37 km), which is representative of the rest of the project. The case study presented is a first of its kind done in the Bank where an effort was made to quantify both social benefits and transport cost savings as part of the evaluation of improving rural access roads.

General Approach

A cost benefit analysis of the project investments has been carried out; its main assumptions and findings are summarized below. Since gathering socio-economic data for each project rural road for purposes of estimating its economic rate of return (ERR) is difficult and expensive, and since these are low-volume roads (less than 30 vehicles per day), the following methodology has been used: for one typical project road (such as the 37 km. Dakpai-Buli road which has the advantage of considerable area-specific socio-economic data collected and analyzed by the Netherlands funding agency NEDA under their integrated development project for the district), its ERR was estimated in detail based on quantification of social and economic benefits.[109] Based on this sample exercise, socio-economic norms and criteria were developed to test the viability of all other project roads.

Cost-Benefit Analysis of Dakpai-Buli Road

Project Benefits: The project roads will provide many types of benefits: (a) it will improve access to social infrastructure (schools and health centers), providing many benefits from increased education and health facilities and improved social interaction and mobility, which are important for social and economic development; (b) it will provide better access to markets by reducing transport costs, and by making it physically feasible for the first time to transport certain types of goods (such as construction materials), since the existing modes of mule transport and porterage are unable to handle such key capital inputs (for construction of houses, schools, small hydro-electric projects) and for general economic development; (c) it will improve the marketability of perishable goods through timely and cheaper transport, and this will provide a direct incentive for more market-oriented agriculture, with more profitable cash crops, and also raise rural income and employment; and (d) it will help isolated rural communities spread over the difficult mountain slopes of the country (home to 85 percent of Bhutan's population and 36 percent of its national income) to remain connected to the national economy. It will prevent their migration to urban areas that do not have the capacity to absorb them. Project impact in all these benefit-categories will be limited primarily to the project areas.

In what follows, an attempt is made to quantify some of the project benefits described above: (a) social benefits, (b) transport cost savings, and (c) agricultural benefits. Other benefits from industrial and regional development will be difficult to quantify and therefore no attempt is made to assess these impacts. A lack of data only permits a partial assessment, resulting in a conservative estimates of project economic return. The analysis focuses on one project road, the Dakpai-Buli road, as discussed above.

Social Benefits: A novel feature of the analysis is quantification of part of the social benefits (in addition to transport cost savings); we have made rough estimates of the value of better access to education which the road will provide, using Bhutanese data on enrollment levels with improved road access, and income levels of educated and uneducated persons. Improved road access (removing the present constraint of about 2 days' walking) will allow easy transport of children to schools, or schools may get located closer to the communities, leading to higher school enrollment levels, and improvement in the quality of schools. RGOB already plans on building new elementary and junior high schools following road construction when transport costs are reduced. Preliminary estimates, based on higher enrollment rates in the more accessible areas in the same district, indicate that about 75-100 children, would additionally go to schools every year if the road is built. More girls would attend because of proximity, and more boys would be released from the task of transporting goods. The life-time earnings of the educated versus uneducated samples provide an estimate of the income differentials. The net incremental income has been assessed after deducting estimated education and continuing education costs. This is attributable as net value added by the road since the additional enrollment would not have happened without the improved access provided by the road. Indeed education (especially education of girls) brings many more social benefits than income benefits, but we limited our estimate to incremental income from education. We have also estimated some health benefits (in reduced sick days, and reduced maternity and other deaths) attributable to improved access to health facilities, based on available local data. Overall, about 30% of the project benefits derive from quantifiable social benefits.

Box E.2.1. *Defining Accessibility in Bhutan*

It should be added that in a region where 2-3 days walking to the nearest road is usual, reducing this to even one day walking distance to/from a road is considered beneficial. Villagers have said that a distance of one day walking allows them to go to the road for sending produce by truck or for other services (often staying with relatives overnight), or for services such as health centers or community schools to be located within such villages. It was mentioned that a common practice is for school children to stay with relatives, if the road/school area is within at least a day's walking distance so that parents can visit them often with food and other supplies. Longer distance is considered too far for such purposes. We have therefore considered villages within a day's walking distance (say 25 km) as falling within the direct beneficiary zone of project roads

Source: Authors.

Transport Cost Savings: Basic traffic data estimates were supported by traffic surveys from the project area (particularly existing mule traffic, and household consumption patterns) conducted by local consultants. Estimates also used traffic growth data gathered during a feeder road project that was completed about five years ago in a similar area of the district. The current traffic level in goods (all traffic that is likely to shift to the road, currently moved as mule traffic or porterage) is about 10 tons per day, which is small. However, with road transport supplanting mule transport, traffic will increase. The estimates assume a traffic growth from about 10 vehicles per day (three trucks, two buses and five light vehicles/pick-ups) for the first year (2002) to about 22 vehicles per day in the fifth year, which is supported both by traffic demand (growth) in the area, and the growth pattern observed after road development in a similar area in the district. These may even be modest assumptions. The unit cost savings will be significant since the alternative cost of mule transport is very high, or about $3 per ton-km (as field surveys and mule tariffs established). This is compared to an estimated trucking cost of about $0.40 per ton-km (assumed high in this terrain).

The transport benefits have been calculated for the following four major categories: (a) transport savings on the normal growth of non-agricultural goods traffic assuming traffic levels without the road project (agricultural traffic is excluded since the benefits from transporting agricultural goods will be indirectly included in the estimate of incremental agricultural income); (b) transport savings on the induced non-agricultural goods traffic (additional non-agricultural traffic induced by the availability of the road); (c) transport savings on the normal growth of passenger traffic (persons traveling in the without road assumption; and (c) transport savings on the induced passenger traffic.

The unit cost savings are significant since the alternative cost of mule transport is very high, about $3.0 equivalent per ton-km (as per field surveys and mule tariff established by RGOB), as against possible trucking cost of about $0.4 per ton-km (assumed high in this terrain) after the road is built. For normal growth in existing traffic, the full reduction in costs is counted as project benefits; for induced traffic, only 50% of net benefits is counted as project benefits. Road transport benefits are assumed frozen at the level reached in 27th year since the road will reach saturation level of traffic at that time; the 27th year level of benefits is continued for the full road life of 40 years.

For normal growth in existing traffic, the full reduction in costs is counted as project benefits. For induced traffic, only 50 percent of net benefits is counted as project benefits. Road transport benefits are assumed frozen at the level reached in the 27th year since the road will reach saturation level of traffic at that time. The 27th year level of benefits is continued for the full road life of 40 years.

Using traffic growth data from a similar road constructed five years earlier in the same district and assuming similar traffic growth, total traffic was assumed (conservatively) to double in five years after completion of the road, reaching about 22 vehicles per day in year five. It is assumed to reach a level of about 100 vehicles per day in year 27. This projected traffic is an aggregation of all traffic (agricultural, non-agricultural, for existing, normal and induced growth).

> **Box E.2.2.** *Avoiding the Error of Double Counting Benefits*
>
> The passenger traffic estimates are modest, since normally passenger traffic growth is found to exceed goods traffic growth in most cases. These figures exclude future bus traffic, if any, of children to/from schools or of people to/from health centers; since education benefits and health benefits are estimated separately on a different basis, we did not want to count their transport savings also as it would have meant double-counting of benefits; moreover such traffic is considered not significant. In the case of agricultural traffic, which is significant, the traffic was considered only for estimating road capacity/saturation levels, but their transport savings were excluded to avoid double-counting of benefits.
>
> *Source:* Authors.

Agricultural Benefits: In terms of the agricultural benefits induced by the road, the estimate is based on a detailed analysis of the present cropping patterns in the area and the likely switch in cropping patterns to more profitable cash crops which will be facilitated by easier access to markets. A farm model with local production and cost co-efficients has been used for this estimate. It estimates the net value added in agricultural production due to reduced transport costs of farm inputs and output, and increased switch-over to cash crops (such as oranges, chilies, and other vegetables), based on similar experiences in other parts of Bhutan. It has been verified that apart from a marginal increase in extension services and the use of more fertilizers and improved seeds, no significant agricultural investments in land improvements would be required for the expected change to marketable crops. The net incremental benefits from agriculture (after meeting all additional costs of farming and transport) have been taken as benefits brought about by the road, since the absence of a road is the main bottleneck in producing more market-oriented crops in this area.

Project Costs

Road construction and maintenance requires major initial investments, followed by periodic maintenance costs. The Dakpai-Buli road is being built from year one (1999) to year three (2001). The first year of full road use is taken as year four (2002), ignoring interim benefits from the partial use of completed road sections. The stream of benefits and costs has been calculated for a 40-year period, (year 2002 to year 2041). This is justified since a well-designed mountain road with low traffic will last much more than 40 years if routine maintenance is done every year, and if periodically major repair works are undertaken. Adequate routine maintenance and a four-year cycle of periodic maintenance has been assumed in the cost stream to ensure a long life for the road. Moreover, Bhutan has a good past record on road maintenance, and community involvement in road maintenance is increasing, which will help sustain the road over a long life. For converting financial costs into economic costs, foreign components (mainly in construction costs) have been converted using c.i.f. (import) prices without adjustments; all other local costs and benefits have been converted into economic (border) prices using a factor of 0.9.

Overview of Results

Table E.2.1 summarizes the results of ERR analysis:

Table E.2.1. *Net Present Value (NPV) of Economic Cost Benefit Streams (at 12 percent discount rate, in thousands of US$)*	
Cost of road investment and maintenance	3,817
Total Benefit attributable to the road	6,244
Transport benefits (non-agricultural traffic)	3,476
Net agricultural benefits	56
Net education benefits	1,699
Net health benefits	113
ERR (base case)	**15.1%**
Source: Authors.	

The main assumptions relate to higher school enrollment levels after road construction; traffic growth and transport savings; agricultural benefits; project life, and maintenance costs are described in the previous chapter.

Sensitivity Analysis / Switching Values of Critical Items: Varying the economic cost and benefit streams of the base case produces the following sensitivity table (Table E.2.2):

Table E.2.2. *Results of Sensitivity Analysis*			
Variations in Cost Stream		Variations in Benefit Stream	
	80%	100%	120%
80%	ERR 15.1%	ERR 16.9%	ERR 18.5%
100%	ERR 13.6%	ERR 15.1%	ERR 16.5%
120%	ERR 12.5%	ERR 13.9%	ERR 15.1%
Source: Authors.			

Varying the economic cost and benefit streams produces the following switching values (at 10 percent and at 12 percent) for the ERR (Table E.2.3):

Table E.2.3. *Switching Values*			
Variations in Cost Stream		Variations in Benefit Stream	
	42%	61%	100%
100%	ERR 10.0%	ERR 12.0%	ERR 15.1%
162%			ERR 12.0%
237%			
Source: Authors.			

The above figures show that the ERR estimates are robust, under varying pessimistic assumptions.

Assumption Regarding the Life of the Road: A separate sensitivity analysis was conducted with regard to the life of the road. The base-case ERR is based on a 40-year life of the road. This is a realistic assumption, because this is a well-designed mountainous road with low traffic—this road should have an even longer life. Moreover, adequate maintenance allocation has been made in the analysis. Bhutan has a good past record of satisfactory road maintenance, and local user community involvement in road maintenance is part of the project design and understanding with RGOB.

For life assumptions of 30 years and 20 years, the base-case ERR will decline to 12.9 percent and 10.1 percent respectively. As noted above, these reduced-life assumptions are not realistic. The results, however, highlight the need for good maintenance policies and practices to ensure viability of such road investments.

Applying the Dakpai-Buli Road ERR Analysis to the Total Project

Dakpai-Buli is considered typical of other project roads. The above analysis shows that the road produces an ERR of above 15 percent for 37 kilometers, costing about $3.6 million and serving about 8000 direct beneficiaries. This amounts to a per capita cost of about $450 in terms of project cost per beneficiary. Based on this, the per capita investment corresponding to 12 percent ERR is about $560. In other words, based on the Dakpai-Buli road impact analysis, a per capita investment per beneficiary of $560 (in 1999 prices mention the base price factor early in your narrative) is considered viable at 12 percent ERR.

In view of the difficulty of repeating such detailed studies for all the project roads, and since the access problems and economic conditions are similar in the service areas of other project roads, the norm of a maximum per capita (per beneficiary) cost of $560 is applied as an acceptable threshold for economic viability. These criteria will need to be satisfied for all project roads. The preliminary analysis for the other project roads shows that the per-capita investment for the remaining project roads will be less than $450, indicating a higher than 15 percent ERR, based on the Dakpai-Buli road norm of Dakpai-Buli road. This indicates that the overall Project ERR would exceed the 15 percent estimated for the Dakpai-Buli Road. More details are given in the project files.

Road Selection Criteria for Project Roads: Based on the above analysis, the following criteria (among others) have been agreed upon with RGOB for the selection of new roads under the project:

(a) Project roads must be part of the list of feeder roads included as priority roads in the ongoing Eighth Five-Year Plan. These road priorities have been decided upon on the basis of extensive participatory discussions involving local communities, district administrations, the Planning Commission and sector Ministries, and the King, who visited all districts for discussions on plan priorities with the local communities. They reflect a participatory, socioeconomic prioritization process, based on national economic and regional development objectives; and

(b) Based on the economic return calculations made for the Dakpai-Buli road, a per capita investment per beneficiary of $560 is considered viable at 12 percent ERR. All project roads should satisfy this criteria. The direct beneficiaries are estimated using the populations from villages that directly benefit from the project (defined as villages within one day's walking distance to or from project road). It can be increased by about 10 percent to include other beneficiaries who would directly benefit from trade with or visits to the newly accessible areas. (This was the procedure followed for the Dakpai-Buli Road). The road construction costs are to be calculated in 1999 prices, including 15 percent physical contingency.

Concluding Remarks

This case study presents an extreme case where (a) the road investment cost is very high at about $100,000 per kilometer, even for a one-lane gravel road (because of mountainous terrain and the decision to use environmentally friendly 'cut and fill methods'); (b) the number of beneficiaries per road is small due to sparse population density (about 8,000 direct beneficiaries); and (c) per capita investment is high, at about $450 per beneficiary (compared to below $100 in other countries).

The case illustrates that by attempting to carefully quantify the true economic costs of present transport bottlenecks, and the socioeconomic benefits which the investment will bring, the project could be justified. The use of realistic mule transport costs in the absence of the project, quantification of social benefits, and the use of realistic 40-year life assumption for the road, have all contributed to the viable ERR estimate, in spite of high investment costs. The 40-year life span assumption for the project road was endorsed by experienced road engineers, since it will be a well-built mountain road with relatively little traffic and good maintenance standards based on the good past road maintenance record of Bhutan.

The detailed studies carried out to assess the socioeconomic benefits were expensive, but can be effectively undertaken on a sample basis to establish an acceptable threshold of investment.

IDA Executive Directors, during Board consideration of the project, commended this new approach in assessing social benefits in rural road projects. The Quality Assurance Group of the Bank, which reviewed the project for quality at entry, also commended it for overall quality, including the innovative methods used in the economic analysis.

One lesson learned concerns estimating separate benefits from net value added in agriculture due to the switch to market-based crops after road construction. This was an elaborate procedure, using farm models from other parts of Bhutan where road availability has induced changes in cropping patterns. However, we later concluded that this exercise was not essential. The ERR estimates would have been almost similar if agricultural traffic was included as part of total traffic, and their benefits assessed using transport cost savings and reasonable traffic growth assumptions. This would have made the analysis much simpler and less time-consuming.

APPENDIX F
LOW VOLUME ROADS ECONOMIC DECISION MODEL (RED)

Introduction

The Low Volume Roads Economic Decision Model (RED) was developed under the Road Maintenance Initiative (RMI), a key component of the Sub-Saharan Africa Transport Policy Program (SSATP), to improve the decision making process for the development and maintenance of low-volume roads. The model performs an economic evaluation of road investments options using the consumer surplus approach and is customized to the characteristics of low-volume roads such as a) the high uncertainty of model inputs, particularly the traffic and condition of unpaved roads; b) the importance of travel time measurements to characterize the condition of unpaved roads and for model validation; c) the need for a comprehensive analysis of generated traffic; and d) the need to clearly define all accrued benefits. RED computes benefits for normal, generated and diverted traffic and takes into account changes in road length, condition, geometry, type, accidents and days per year when the passage of vehicles is further disrupted by a highly deteriorated road condition (wet season). Users can add other benefits or costs to the analysis, such as non-motorized traffic, social services and environmental impacts, if computed separately. The model is presented on a series of Excel 5.0 workbooks that collect all user inputs, present the results in an efficient manner, and perform sensitivity, switching values, and stochastic risk analyses. RED is available at the World Bank Road Software Tools Internet site:

http://www.worldbank.org/html/fpd/transport/roads/tools.htm

Sample Model Applications

Two typical RED applications are presented, which consist of the economic justification of surfacing a gravel road and justifying maintenance expenditures needed to maintain a certain level of service.

Surfacing a Gravel Road: A two-lane gravel road, with 200 vehicles per day, receives maintenance that consists of grading every 90 days and regravelling every 5 years, which yields a road with good passability and average roughness equal to 11.0 IRI. RED is used to evaluate the following project-options: (a) rehabilitate the road and improve the maintenance policy increasing the grading frequency to one grading every 60 days, (b) upgrade the road to surface treatment standard, and (c) surface the road with concrete blocks. The basic inputs are given in Table F.1 below.

Table F.1. *Inputs for Example No. 1*				
	Without Project	Project-Option 1	Project-Option-2	Project-Option 3
Description	Grading every 90 days	Grading every 60 days	Surface Treatment Surface	Concrete Block Surface
Average roughness (IRI)	11.0	9.0	3.5	5.0
Investment cost ($/km)		15,000	125,000	48,000
Maintenance costs ($/km/year)	4,200	4,800	1,000	2,400
Source: Authors.				

Option 1 investment cost is the regravelling cost and options 2 and 3 investment costs are the paving costs, considering a 6.5 m wide surface treatment road and a 4.0 m wide concrete block road. The future maintenance costs needed to maintain the defined levels of service are estimated for each case. The analysis period is 10 years, discount rate is 12 percent and economic to financial costs multiplier is 0.85. The price elasticity of demand for transport is set to 1.0 for all vehicles, meaning that a one percent decrease in transport costs yields a one percent increase in generated traffic due to reduction in transport costs.

The results, given in Table F.2 below, show that options 1 and 3 are economically justified with a rate of return greater than 12.0 percent, while option 2 (upgrade the road to a surface treatment standard) is not justified, at the given discount rate of 12 percent, mainly to the relatively low traffic and high investment costs.

Table F.2. *Results of RED Analysis*			
	Option 1	Option 2	Option 3
Internal rate of return	24%	10%	33%
IRR sensitivity:			
Normal traffic x 0.75	15%	5%	24%
Investment costs x 1.25	18%	5%	25%
Maintenance costs x 1.25	15%	10%	31%
Source: Authors.			

Rehabilitating the gravel road has positive economic benefits, but this option is fairly responsive to changes in the future maintenance policy, and the corresponding maintenance costs. Therefore, there should be some assurance that the road agency has the capacity to maintain the road before the rehabilitation is implemented. The option of surfacing the road with concrete blocks has the highest rate of return (33 percent) and under the sensitivity scenarios it maintains a high rate of return. Therefore, it is an economically robust option. This evaluation considers a 4.0 meter-wide concrete block road, but if one considers a 6.5 meter-wide concrete block road, at a cost of 78,000 $/km, the rate of return drops to 14 percent. A switching values analysis indicates that the daily traffic should be 180 vehicles per day to marginally justify a 6.5 meter-wide concrete block road and 90 vehicles per day to marginally justify a 4.0 meter-wide concrete block road. Note that these results are for a particular set of road user costs, traffic growth rates and condition of the road under the without project case. Therefore, the results can not be generalized.

Justifying Maintenance Expenditures: A two-lane earth road with 40 vehicles per day is in bad condition with average car speeds of 45 km/hour during most of the year and 35 km/hour during 30 days of the year (wet season). The road agency proposes to improve the level of service by eliminating the critical days and increasing the average car speeds to 55 km/hour during all year. The basic inputs are given in Table F.3 below.

Table F.3. *Inputs for Example No. 2*

	Without Project	With Project
Car speeds (km/hour)	45	55
Critical passability days	30	0
Car speeds during critical days	35	NA

Source: Authors.

RED is used to evaluate the level of annual maintenance expenditures economically justified to achieve the proposed level of service. In the without project scenario, the road agency annual maintenance expenditures are $700/km per year for routine maintenance and one grading per year. RED finds that the maximum annual maintenance expenditures economically justified to achieve the proposed level of service is $3,400/km per year. The results, found in Table F.4, are the following.

Table F.4. *Results of RED Analysis*

	Without Project	With Project
Maintenance costs ($/km/year)	700	3,400
Internal rate of return (%)	NA	12.0%

Source: Authors.

This means that that to achieve the level of service of 55 km/hour speeds all year, annual expenditures should not be more that $3,400/km per year for the given 40 vehicles per day. To achieve this level of service, the agency proposes a maintenance policy of routine maintenance, regravelling every seven years and three gradings per year, which amounts to $3,700/km per year. The proposed expenditures ($3,700) are higher than the estimated maximum economically allowable expenditures ($3,400), but the agency proceeds with the proposed policy because the difference ($300) is considered to be covered by the other social benefits not included in the analysis.

Conclusions

The model is easy to use, flexible, and requires a limited number of input data requirements consistent with the level of data collection needed for low-volume roads. The model is used to evaluate road investments and maintenance of low-volume roads and it estimates benefits to road users, to which other benefits can be added. Particular attention was given to the presentation of the results, highlighting all input assumptions. Because of the high variability and uncertainty regarding low-volume roads, emphasis was placed on the sensitivity, switching values and risk analysis.

NOTES

1. See Malmberg Calvo 1998.

2. Both under preparation. To be published in 2001.

3. Particularly for maintenance, the support of central government can rarely be relied upon. Exceptions are some road funds and other transfer mechanisms. See Christina Malmberg Calvo.

4. In some cases, at steep hills (see Appendix B) or where suitable gravel material cannot be found (as in Bangladesh), paving may be the most economical solution.

5. Often justified based on anticipated lack of maintenance and a lack of willingness to tackle this problem.

6. This approach is further elaborated upon in Chapter 4 and Appendix E.

7. Poverty Net: *http://www.worldbank.org/poverty/data/trends/index.htm*.

8. "Designated" means formal government responsibility or ownership has been established.

9. See Malmberg Calvo 1998.

10. Barwell 1996.

11. The authors estimate that of the 3 billion rural population in developing countries, 30 percent (900 million) are living in villages without reliable access, while 10 percent (300 million) are not provided with motorized access at all. To improve access to these people, an estimated $40 billion of investment and an annual $1 billion in maintenance would be required.

12. During the 1970s and 1980s many so-called integrated rural development projects were executed, supporting various sub-sectors. Most of them failed because they were not delivered in a manner consistent with national or local institutional and financial frameworks.

13. PAD Nepal Road Maintenance and Development Project 1999.

14. PAD Bhutan Rural Access Project 1999.

15. Rural household survey conducted in preparation of the Rural Roads Component of the Andhra Pradesh Economic Restructuring Project 1997.

16. Pankaj 1999.

17. Adapted from World Bank 1996a.

18. Volume I (Malmberg Calvo) was published in 1998. Volume II is this paper. Volumes III and IV are planned to be published in 2001.

19. For example, see the Comprehensive Development Framework (CDF) or Poverty Reduction Strategy Papers (PRSP) at: *http://www.worldbank.org/*

20. "Rural Transport Projects: Concept Development, Justification, and Appraisal," a lecture series given by Prof. John Howe at the World Bank, September 20-24, 1999.

21. Intermediate means of transport not only include non-motorized means of transport (NMT) such as bicycles and animal drawn carts, but also appropriate low-cost motorized means of transport such as scooters and single-axle tractors.

22. See Barwell 1996.

23. For example, see Malmberg Calvo 1998.

24. Geoff Edmonds (1998): *Wasted Time: The Price of Poor Access.*

25. Avoiding some transport needs altogether, for example, through improved communications, is a promising and cost-effective alternative.

26. Refer to Education Advisory Services, World Bank.

27. The topic is being addressed in a World Bank Technical Paper entitled "Developing Rural Transport Policies and Strategies," planned for publication in 2001.

28. Often projects "assign" responsibilities to communities (in the absence of local government capacity) which exceed their capacity in the long-run, or which are too complicated to manage (for example, links that provide access to several villages). This is often done instead of the necessary, but difficult, task of promoting capacity building at local government and community levels.

29. See Malmberg Calvo 1998.

30. For example, in Ghana, rural roads are managed by the Department of Feeder Roads of the Ministry of Roads and Highways in collaboration with local governments. Similar arrangements exist in Bangladesh and India.

31. This will require a one-hour walk from the village to the most remote part of the community road and one hour back, which reduces the available effective work time for maintenance to six hours. However, in countries with a low population density, community RTI is often much longer than five km (which often means that roads are not affordable).

32. See Note 21.

33. In some countries, such as France, access is stated as a fundamental human right in the constitution.

34. Many roads are being upgraded to higher standards at (despite negative rates of return) or (despite dubious measurements of their development effectiveness and economic profitability), Therefore, the potential for the reallocation of resources to basic access exists. However, if real transport bottlenecks are observed (such as congested or heavily deteriorated high-traffic roads), these can be economically very costly and need to be addressed in priority.

35. As in the case of Bangladesh where non-motorized rickshaw-vans (for goods) and passenger rickshaws dominate traffic.

36. In the rare cases where transfer arrangements from central budgets or road funds exist for financing RTI maintenance, local communities must still provide substantial contributions. This is one of the main reasons for local level ownership through a participatory approach to planning, monitoring and evaluation for this type of intervention.

37. Some empirical evidence from recent World Bank projects (see Appendix E) suggests that the limit of what can be afforded in terms of RTI investment is close to the annual per capita GDP of the population served.

38. If a country is not maintaining its main road network, it is also unlikely to be maintaining its secondary road network and new public investments should be avoided.

39. For example, in Burkina Faso the existing path network (that provides access to all the rural households) has been estimated at 112,000 kilometers. If this network would be developed to roads and added to the existing road network of 16,000 kilometers, the road density of Burkina Faso would be comparable to that of a developed country with similar population density.

40. See Note 11.

41. See Notes 13, 14 and 15.

42. For example, in Burkina Faso, Gnanderman 1999, found that there are about 112,000 km of paths versus 16,000 km of roads.

43. Normally designed for ten or twenty year flood levels.

44. Up to a traffic range of 50-150 VPD, "full access" will normally require a gravel road of one-and-a-half lanes (carriageway width of 4.5 to 5.5 meters), while above 150 VPD, a two-lane road will be appropriate (6 meters carriageway with shoulders). The provision of a bituminous sealed surface (double/triple surface dressing or OTTA seals) is usually only justified at traffic levels of above 200 to 400 vehicles per day, depending on terrain, rainfall, and soils. In India, the "standard" full access rural road is a single-lane road with a carriageway width of 3.6 meters, a formation width of 7.5 meters, and a surface layer of 40

cm consisting of a 2 cm bituminous layer on a triple layer of water-bound macadam and a gravel layer costing a total of $40,000 equivalent per kilometer.

45. "Road Building in the Tropics," TRL 1993.

46. See Note 41.

47. In India, the policy is that rural road closures should not exceed 12 hours per event and not more than 15 days per year in total. In most francophone African countries, the road agencies operate rain barriers on rural roads. Normally, the rule is that these barriers must be closed during heavy rains and at least four hours thereafter. In Nepal, due to the severity of the monsoon season and the high cost of permanent river crossings, most roads other than the national highways and urban roads are seasonal access roads that are closed for about three months during the monsoon season.

48. However, in the USA, about 40 percent of the approximately 6 million kilometer road network are gravel or earth roads and are in their majority single-lane (Highway Statistics 1998, Federal Highway Administration).

49. See Richard Robinson.

50. For example, new lending instruments, such as the World Bank's Adaptable Program Lending programs, allow for a longer-term performance-based approach to project lending.

51. For example, the SRR (Structures on Rural Roads) component of the first and second Rural Roads and Market Improvement Projects of the World Bank in Bangladesh, and the Morogoro Road Support Project assisted by the Swiss Development Cooperation in Tanzania.

52. The National Transport Program Support Project, 2000. Also see, Asif Faiz et al. TRB Record.

53. However, a "phased" approach can be recommended, as practiced in the "Green Road Approach" in Nepal, where first a trail is constructed and then gradually expanded to a road, particularly in a mountainous environment.

54. For example, see Heggie and Vickers 1998.

55. As demonstrated by Ellis and Hine, "a road with traffic of 10 vehicles per day has 0.05 conflicts per day at a speed of 40 km/h. This will increase to 1.3 conflicts per day at a volume of 50 vehicles per day."

56. Although encroachment into existing alignment is a situation encountered frequently.

57. For environmentally friendly RTI design, see Appendix B, particularly the chapter on bio-engineering.

58. OP/BP/GP 4.01 Environmental Assessment and OP/BP/GP 4.30 Involuntary Resettlement; *Roads and the Environment*, WB Technical Paper 376, 1997; and *Managing the Social Dimension of Transport. The Role of Social Assessment.* World Bank, Social Development Web site.

59. For example, the "Destitute Women Program" implemented in Bangladesh.

60. Good guidelines for the training of small scale contractors can be found in a ILO publication: *Capacity Building for Contracting in the Construction Sector*.

61. See Stock and de Veen 1996.

62. See Bentall, Beusch and de Veen 1999.

63. See Malmberg Calvo 1998.

64. See Larcher 1999.

65. See MART Working Papers Nos. 1 to 14.

66. World Bank. 1994. *Bank-Financed Projects with Community Participation: A Manual for Designing Procurement and Disbursement Mechanisms*. Africa Technical Department, Washington, DC.

67. As a rule of thumb, expenditures for maintenance should be 50-80 percent of total expenditures for roads in a growing network and 90-95 percent in a mature network.

68. See Malmberg Calvo 1998.

69. In Burkina Faso, for example, the systematic execution of grading operations in combination with spot recharging of gravel has greatly reduced the need for periodic regravelling.

70. Hine, J and Cundill, M. "Economic assessment of road projects: Do our current procedures tell us what we want to know?" International Workshop On Impact Evaluation and Analysis of Transportation Projects In Developing Countries. Bombay, December, 1994.

71. Tsunokawa and Hoban 1997; Beenhakker 1987; Chapter 4, Handbook of Economic Analysis in Transport Project Work.

72. For more on participatory approaches see World Bank, Social Development web site: *http://www.worldbank.org* – Topics and Sectors – Social Development.

73. For further information on participatory planning tools see Malmberg Calvo 1998.

74. For more information on participatory techniques see World Bank Participation Source Book, 1996.

75. A good example are the guidelines and Thana Planning Handbook prepared by the Local Government Engineering Department (LGED) in Bangladesh.

76. A low-cost survey should assess the existing level of access and determine the types of interventions necessary to secure basic access. A small team (driver, engineer, local foreman) with vehicle should be able to survey around 40km/day of roads, or 20km/day of paths on foot or by means of IMT.

77. Basic access is understood here as defined in Chapter 3 and elaborated in Appendixes B and C.

78. For example, in the province of Saskatchewan in Canada, wheat farms are based on square mile lots. Along the perimeter of the lot, there is normally a public access road from which a penetration road leads to the farm house. When selecting which of these access roads should be gravelled (which means the provision of costly "crusher-run" material because the in-situ soils are mainly clays) it has been decided that, per farm, only one access road to the main road system (and normally the shortest one) is being gravelled (and therefore becomes an all-season road) while the others remain seasonal earth roads. This is an example of a "basic access" approach that has been applied in a developed country.

79. World Bank, OP 10.04 1994.

80. Normally, life cycle costs should be used in this formula (including maintenance). However, in this case, maintenance costs were found to be uniform over the network and there was no need to consider them..

81. The cost of upgrading of all link that cost less than $50 per person served would exhaust the available budget.

82. For a further discussion, see Gannon and Lebo 1999.

83. The producer surplus (PS) method has been widely applied throughout the developing world, especially where road improvements are intended to increase agricultural value added. This method was codified in the work of Carnemark, Biderman and Bovet (1976), and later expanded and simplified by Beenhakker and Lago (1983).

84. For example, see Padeco (1996), Non-Motorized Transport (NMT) Modeling in HDM-4, Draft Final Report for Transport Division of the World Bank. Also see World Bank (1996), Bangladesh, Second Rural Roads and Markets Improvement and Maintenance Project, Project Implementation Document No. 15, Economic Appraisal of FRB Roads, South Asia Regional Office, World Bank.

85. For additional information on valuing travel time savings, see Gwilliam 1997.

86. See Cook 1990.

87. R. Ahmed and M. Hosain, Development Impact of Rural Infrastructure in Bangladesh. International Food Policy Research Institute (IFPRI) in collaboration with Bangladesh Institute of Development Studies (BIDS), 1990.

88. World Bank. 1999. Project Appraisal Document—Kingdom of Bhutan, Rural Access Project. South Asia Regional Office, Washington, DC.

89 As elaborated in Chapter 3 of this paper, basic access roads provide all-season access (within certain limits) to the prevailing vehicles. Traffic levels on basic access roads are less than 50 motorized, four-wheeled vehicles per day, but often there is a substantial amount of NMT.

90. TRL Road Note No. 6: *A Guide to Geometric Design* and TRL publication: *Road Building in the Tropics*.

91. Paige-Green, P and A Bam. *Passability criteria for unpaved roads*. Research Report RR 91/172, Department of Transport, South Africa, 1994; also Ellis, SD and JL Hine. *Rapid appraisal techniques for identifying maintenance priorities on low volume rural roads*. Unpublished Project Report PR/OSC/122/97, Transport Research Laboratory, 1998.

92. An equivalent laboratory test would be an unsoaked CBR of 15 percent with modified proctor compaction.

93. See Box B.1

94. *A Guide to Geometric Design*, TRL Overseas Road Note 6, Transport Research Laboratory, Crowthorne, 1988 defines the three categories as follows:

    Level (0 to 10 five-meter ground contours per km): Level or gently rolling terrain with largely unrestricted horizontal and vertical alignment.

    Rolling (11 to 25 five-meter ground contours per km): Rolling terrain with low hills introducing moderate levels of rise and fall with some restrictions on vertical alignment.

    Mountainous (greater than 25 five-meter ground contours per km). Rugged, hilly and mountainous with substantial restrictions in both horizontal and vertical alignment.

95. *Principles of Low-Cost Road Engineering in Mountainous Regions*, TRL Overseas Road Note 16, Transport Research Laboratory, Crowthorne, 1997.

96. Bridges are normally designed to accommodate annual high flows without excessively restricting flow or incurring damage either to the structure or surrounding land. A high flood which may only occur once in every 100 years may cause damage to approach embankments but should not damage the superstructure. See: *A Design Manual for Small Bridges*, Overseas Road Note 9, Transport and Road Research Laboratory.

97. Nepal 1997.

98. National Research Council, Washington DC, 1993. *Vetiver Grass, a Thin Line Against Erosion.*

99. Clark, J., and J. Hellin. *Bio-engineering for Effective Road Maintenance in the Caribbean.* Natural Resources Institute, Chatham. 1996.

100. Bentall P., A. Beusch and J. de Veen 1999.

101. Extracted from Stock A., and J. de Veen 1996.

102. ATBrief 8, Improving Paths and Tracks in *Appropriate Technology,* Vol. 21 No. 1, gives more details on these approaches.

103. Wagner et al. 1992. *Survey, Design, and Construction of Trail Suspension Bridges for Remote Areas*, Volumes A to E, SKAT. Switzerland.

104. These "weights" are based on the standard measure of road capacity, Passenger Car Units (PCU), an approach applied on higher-category roads, which allows consistent comparison of traffic throughout the network. However, for RTI where traffic capacity is not usually an issue, the merit of this conversion is not clear.

105. For details on the rural road master planning process, see World Bank Infrastructure Notes, Transport No. RT-4, January 2000.

106. While the appropriateness of using IRI for rural road project evaluation remains debatable, for this particular project, it is judged appropriate by the project team, given the substantial differences in roughness found among different types of rural road and the relative uniformity within each type of rural road in the area.

107. (1) See PADECO (1996), *Non-Motorized Transport (NMT) Modeling in HDM-4*, Draft Final Report for Transport Division of the World Bank. (2) World Bank (1996), *Bangladesh: Second Rural Roads and Markets Improvement and Maintenance Project: Project Implementation Document No. 15: Economic Appraisal of FRB Roads*, South Asia Regional Office, World Bank.

108. The main economic analysis and report was done by a team consisting of Thampil Pankaj, and Eddy Bynens, with considerable support from Kynghkhor consultants of Bhutan who conducted various field studies and some of the analysis. The study received valuable guidance from Frannie Léautier, and support and advice from Juan Gaviria and other Bank colleagues. The detailed study is available from the World Bank's Rural Roads Thematic Group Web site at *http://www.worldbank.org/html/fpd/transport/rt_over.htm*.

BIBLIOGRAPHY

Ahmed, R., and M. Hosain. 1990. "Development Impact of Rural Infrastructure in Bangladesh." International Food Policy Research Institute (IFPRI) in collaboration with Bangladesh Institute of Development Studies (BIDS).

Airey, T., and G. Taylor. 1999. "Prioritization Procedure for Improvement of Very Low-Volume Roads." *Transportation Research Record* 1652, Transportation Research Board, Washington, D.C.

Ali-Nejadfard, F. 2000. *Rural Accessibility Planning.* ASIST Bulletin 10. http://www.ilo.org/asist.

Andersson, C., A. Beusch, and D. Miles. 1996. *Road Maintenance and Regravelling (ROMAR): Using Labour-Based Methods.* International Labour Organization, Geneva.

Archondo-Callao, R., and A. Faiz. 1994. *Estimating Vehicle Operating Costs.* World Bank Technical Paper 234. Washington, D.C.

Archondo-Callao, R. 1999. "Roads Economic Decision Model (RED) for Economic Evaluation of Low Volume Roads." Sub-Saharan Africa Transport Policy Program Technical Note No. 18. World Bank, Africa Regional Office, Washington, D.C.

Bangladesh Local Government Engineering Department. 1999. "Bangladesh Rural Infrastructure Impact Study, with special reference to RDP-7 and other projects." Socio-economic Monitoring and Environmental Research, Dhaka.

Banjo, G., and R. Robinson. 1999. "Rural Transport Policies and Strategies." Draft Rural Travel and Transport Program Approach Paper. World Bank, Africa Regional Office, Washington, D.C.

Barwell, Ian. 1996. *Transport and the Village.* World Bank Discussion Paper 344. Washington, D.C.

Beenhakker, H., and A. Lago. 1983. "Economic Appraisal of Rural Roads: Simplified Operational Procedures for Screening and Appraisal." Staff Working Paper 610. World Bank, Washington, D.C.

Beenhakker, H., et al. 1987. *Rural Transport Services: A Guide to Their Planning and Implementation.* London: Intermediate Technologies Publications.

Bentall, P., A. Beusch, and J. de Veen. 1999. *Employment Intensive Infrastructure Programmes: Capacity Building for Contracting in the Construction Sector.* International Labour Organization, Development and Policies Department, Geneva.

Beusch, A., P. Hartmann, R.C. Petts, and P. Winkelmann. 1997. *Low Cost Road Construction in Indonesia: Labour-Based Road Projects in Manggarai District.* Bern: Intercooperation.

Bryceson, D.B. 1995. *Wishful Thinking – Theory and Practise of Western Donor Efforts to Raise the Women's Standard in Rural Africa.* In Bryceson (ed.): *Women Wielding the Hoe: Lessons from Rural Africa for Feminist Theory and Development Practice.* Oxford: Berg Publishers.

Carnemark, C., J. Biderman, and D. Bovet. 1976. "The Economic Analysis of Rural Road Projects." Staff Working Paper 241. World Bank, Washington, D.C.

Carney, D. 1998. "Sustainable Rural Livelihoods: What Contribution Can We Make?" Paper presented at the Department for International Development's National Resources Advisers' Conference, London, U.K, July 1998.

Clark, J., and J. Hellin. 1996. *Bio-engineering for Effective Road Maintenance in the Caribbean*. Natural Resources Institute, Chatham.

Connerly, E. and L. Schroeder. 1996. "Rural Transport Planning." Sub-Saharan Africa Transport Policy Program Working Paper 19. World Bank and Economic Commission for Africa, Washington, D.C.

Cook, C. 1983. "Review of Research on Personal Mobility in Rural Areas of the Developing World." Paper presented at the 25th Annual Meeting of the Transportation Research Forum, Washington, D.C., 1983.

Cook, P. and C. Cook. 1990. "Methodological Review of the Analyses of Rural Transportation Impacts in Developing Countries." *Transportation Research Record* 1274, Transportation Research Board, Washington,.D.C.

Dennis, R. 1998. *Rural Transport and Accessibility, A Synthesis Paper*. International Labour Organization, Development Policies Department, Geneva.

Department for International Development (DFID). 1998. *Sustainable Rural Livelihood: What Contribution Can We Make?* London.

Department for International Development (DFID). 1999. *Local Level Planning and Investment Prioritisation* Final Report. Department for International Development, London and International Labour Organization/ASIST, Geneva.

Department for International Development (DFID). 1999. *Sustainable Livelihoods: Lessons from Early Experience*. London.

Deutsche Gesellschaft für Technische Zusammenarbeit (GTZ) GmbH. 1999. "Rural Transport and Sustainability." Transport Working Paper 2a. Eschborn, Germany.

Devres, Inc. 1980. *Socio-Economic and Environmental Impacts of Low Volume Rural Roads: A Review of the Literature*. A.I.D. Program Evaluation Discussion Paper 7. Office of Evaluation, Bureau for Program and Policy Coordination, Agency for International Development, Washington, D.C.

Dixou-Fyle, K. 1998. *Accessibility Planning and Local Development*. International Labour Organization, Development Policies Department, Geneva.

Doran, J. 1996. *Rural Transport*. Energy and Environment Technology Source Books. London: Intermediate Technology Publications in association with the United Nations Development Fund for Women (UNIFEM), New York.

Edmonds, G. 1998. *Wasted Time: The Price of Poor Access*. International Labour Organization, Development Policies Department, Geneva.

Ellis, S.D., and J.L. Hine. 1998. "The Provision of Rural Transport Services." Sub-Saharan Africa Transport Policy Program Working Paper 37. World Bank, Africa Regional Office, Washington, D.C.

Ellis, S.D., and J.L. Hine. 1998. "Rapid Appraisal Techniques for Identifying Maintenance Priorities on Low Volume Rural Roads." Unpublished Project Report PR/OSC/122/97. Transport Research Laboratory, Crowthorne, Berkshire.

Federal Highway Administration. 1998. Highway Statistics. Washington, D.C.

Gannon, C., and Z. Liu. 1997. "Poverty and Transport". Transportation Water and Urban Development Discussion Paper 30. World Bank, Transport Division, Washington, D.C.

Gannon, C., and J. Lebo. 1999. "Design and Evaluation of Very Low-Volume Rural Roads in Developing Countries." *Transportation Research Record* 1652, Transportation Research Board, Washington, D.C.

Gnandermann, S. 1999. "Etude Preparatoire en voie de l'Elaboration d'une Strategie Gouvernementale des Transports en Milieu Rural." Cellule de Coordination et de Suivi du PASEC-T, Ouagadougou, Burkina Faso.

Greenstein, J. 1993. "Issues Related to Administration of Low-Volume Roads in Developing Countries." *Transportation Research Record* 1426, Transportation Research Board, Washington, D.C.

Gwilliam, K. 1997. "The Value of Time in Economic Evaluation of Transport Projects: Lessons from Recent Research." Transportation, Water and Urban Development Department Infrastructure Note OT-5. World Bank, Transport Division, Washington, D.C.

Hajj H., and V. Setty Pendakur. 2000. "Roads Improvement for Poverty Alleviation in China." Working Paper 1. World Bank, East Asia and Pacific Region, Washington, D.C.

Hancox, W., and R. Petts. 1999. *Guidelines for the Development of Small-Scale Tractor-Based Enterprises in the Rural and Transport Sectors.* Department for International Development, London.

Heggie, I., and P. Vickers. 1998. *Commercial Management and Financing of Roads.* World Bank Technical Paper 409. Washington, D.C.

Hine, J. and M. Cundill. 1994. "Economic assessment of road projects: Do our current procedures tell us what we want to know?" International workshop on Impact Evaluation and Analysis of Transport Projects in Developing Countries, Bombay, December 1994.

Howe, J. 1997. *Transport for the Poor or Poor Transport?* International Labour Organization, Geneva.

Howe, J. 1997. "Least-Cost Planning Methodologies in Rural Transport." Working Paper T&RE 19. International Institute for Infrastructural, Hydraulic and Environmental Engineering, Delft. Holland.

Howe, J. 1999. "Rural Transport Projects: Concept Development, Justification and Appraisal." Lecture Series at the World Bank, September 20-24, 1999.

Hindson, J. 1996. *Earth Roads: Their Construction and Maintenance*. London: Intermediate Technology Publications.

International Road Federation. 2000. World Road Statistics. Washington, D.C.

Kumar, A., and P. Kumar. 1999. "User-Friendly Model for Planning Rural Roads," *Transportation Research Record* 1652, Transportation Research Board, Washington, D.C.

Larcher, P. 1998. *Labour-Based Road Construction*. London: Intermediate Technology Publications.

Larcher, P. 1999. "A Model for a Contractor Support Agency." Management of Appropriate Technology (MART) Working Paper 14. Institute of Development Engineering, Loughborough University, Leicestershire.

Larcher, P., and R. Petts. 1996. "Selective Experience of Training, Contracting and Use of Intermediate Equipment for Labour-Based Roadworks." Management of Appropriate Technology (MART) Working Paper 2. Institute of Development Engineering, Loughborough University, Leicestershire.

Liu, Zhi. 2000. "Economic Analysis of a Rural Basic Access Road Project: The Case of Andhra Pradesh, India." Transportation, Water and Urban Development Department Infrastructure Note RT-5. World Bank, Transport Division, Washington, D.C.

Malmberg Calvo, C. 1998. *Options for Managing and Financing Rural Transport Infrastructure*. World Bank Technical Paper 411. Washington, D.C.

Meyer, W.P., B.N. Acharya, R. Aryal, and B. Karmacharya. 1999. *Green Roads in Nepal, Best Practices Report, 2nd Edition*. Deutsche Gesellschaft für Technische Zusammenarbeit (GTZ) GmbH and Swiss Agency for Development and Cooperation, Kathmandu, Nepal.

Miles, D. 1996. *Towards Guidelines for Labour-Based Contracting*. Working Paper 1. Management of Appropriate Technology, Leicestershire in association with International Labour Organization, Geneva.

Millard, S. 1993. *Road Building in the Tropics, State of the Art Review, 9*. Transport Research Laboratory, Crowthorne, Berkshire.

National Research Council. 1993. *Vetiver Grass, a Thin Line Against Erosion*. Washington D.C.

Nepal, Ministry of Works and Transport, Department of Roads, Geo-environmental Unit. 1997. *Use of Bio-engineering and Bio-engineering Information*.

PADECO Co., Ltd. 1996. "Non-Motorized Transport (NMT) Modeling in HDM-4." (Draft Final Report). Report prepared for World Bank, Transportation, Water and Urban Development Department, Washington, D.C.

Paige-Green, P., and A. Bam. 1994. *Passability Criteria for Unpaved Roads*. Research Report RR 91/172. Department of Transport, South Africa.

Pankaj, T. 1991. "Designing Low-cost Rural Transport Components to Reach the Poor." Transportation, Water and Urban Development Infrastructure Note RD-3. World Bank, Transport Division, Washington, DC

Pankaj, T. 1999. "Socio-Economic Impact of Rural Roads in South Asia: Evidence from Studies and Lessons of Experience." Presentation at the XXIst World Road Congress, Kuala Lumpur, October 5, 1999.

Riverson, J., J. Gaviria, and S. Thriscutt. 1991. *Rural Roads in Sub-Saharan Africa*. World Bank Technical Paper 141. Washington, D.C.

Robinson, R., M.S. Snaith, and Uno Danielson. 1998. *Road Maintenance Management, Concepts and Systems*. London: Macmillan.

Schelling, D., and Z. Liu. 2000. Designing a Rural Basic Access Road Project: The Case of Andhra Pradesh, India. Transportation, Water and Urban Development Infrastructure Note RT-4. World Bank, Transport Division, Washington, D.C.

Schliessler, A. 1993. *Roads: A New Approach for Road Network Management and Conservation*. United Nations Economic Commission for Latin America and the Caribbean, Santiago, Chile.

Sieber, N. 1997. *An Annotated Bibliography on Rural Transport*. The International Forum for Rural Transport and Development, London.

Starkey P. 1999. "Intermediate Means of Transport: People, Paradoxes and Progress." Paper Prepared for an RTTP-organized Workshop on IMT in Kenya, June 1999.

Stock, E. 1995. "Labor-Based Road Rehabilitation: Can Employment Generation be Combined with Private Sector Delivery? The Ghana Experience." Sub-Saharan Africa Transport Policy Program Newsletter 11. World Bank, Africa Regional Office, Washington, D.C.

Stock, A. and J. de Veen. 1996. *Expanding Labor-based Methods for Road Works in Africa*. World Bank Technical Paper 347. Washington, D.C.

Tajgmann, D. and J. de Veen. 1998. *Employment Intensive Infrastructure Programmes: Labour Policies and Practices*. International Labour Organization, Development Policies Department, Geneva.

Taylor, G. 1994. "Improving Paths and Tracks." ATBrief 8. *Appropriate Technology* (21) 1, June 1994. IT Transport, Ardington, Oxfordshire.

Transport and Road Research Laboratory. 1988. *A Guide to Geometric Design*. Overseas Road Note 6. TRL, Crowthorne, Berkshire.

Transport and Road Research Laboratory. 1988. *A Guide to Road Project Appraisal*. Overseas Road Note 5. TRL, Crowthorne, Berkshire.

Transport and Road Research Laboratory. 1992. *A Design Manual for Small Bridges*. Overseas Road Note 9. TRL, Crowthorne, Berkshire.

Transport and Road Research Laboratory. 1993. *A Guide to the Structural Design of Bitumen-Surfaced Roads in Tropical and Subtropical Countries*. Overseas Road Note 31. TRL, Crowthorne, Berkshire.

Transport and Road Research Laboratory. 1997. *Principles of Low Cost Road Engineering in Mountainous Regions*. Overseas Road Note 16. TRL, Crowthorne, Berkshire.

Tsunokawa, K. and C. Hoban (ed.). 1997. *Roads and the Environment: A Handbook*. World Bank Technical Paper 376. Washington, D.C.

Van de Walle, D. 2000. "Choosing Pro-Poor Rural Road Investments." Draft Paper. World Bank, Development Research Group, Washington, D.C.

Wagner, A. et al. 1992. *Survey, Design, and Construction of Trail Suspension Bridges for Remote Areas*, Volumes A to E. Swiss Centre for Development Cooperation in Technology and Management (SKAT), St. Gallen.

Winkelman, P. 1999. *Self-Help for Road Construction: When it Applies—How it can be Encouraged and Supported. Experience in Flores, East Indonesia and Other Countries*. IC Technical Report No 2. Bern: Intercooperation.

World Bank. 1994. Operational Policies (OP) 10.04, *Economic Evaluation of Investment Operations*. Washington, D.C.

World Bank. 1994. *Bank-Financed Projects with Community Participation: A Manual for Designing Procurement and Disbursement Mechanisms*. Africa Technical Department. Washington, D.C.

World Bank. 1996. *Sustainable Transport: Priorities for Policy Reform*. Development in Practice Series. Washington, D.C.

World Bank. 1996. *The World Bank Participation Sourcebook*. Washington, D.C.

World Bank. 1998. "Economic Analysis in Transport Project Work." World Bank, Transport Economic and Sector Policy Thematic Group, Washington, D.C.

World Bank. 1999. *Managing the Social Dimension of Transport. The Role of Social Assessment*. World Bank, Social Assessment Thematic Team, Washington, D.C.

World Bank. 1999. *Vietnam Second Rural Transport Project*. Project Appraisal Document. East Asia and Pacific Regional Office, Washington, D.C.

World Bank. 1999. *Nepal Road Maintenance and Development Project*. Project Appraisal Document. South Asia Regional Office, Washington, D.C.

World Bank. 1999. *Bhutan Rural Access Project*. Project Appraisal Document. South Asia Regional Office, Washington, D.C.

World Bank. 1999. World Development Indicators Database. Washington, D.C.

World Bank. 1996. *Bangladesh Rural Infrastructure Strategy Study*. Dhaka: University Press.

Distributors of World Bank Group Publications

Prices and credit terms vary from country to country. Consult your local distributor before placing an order.

ARGENTINA
World Publications SA
Av. Cordoba 1877
1120 Ciudad de Buenos Aires
Tel: (54 11) 4815-8156
Fax: (54 11) 4815-8156
E-mail: wpbooks@infovia.com.ar

AUSTRALIA, FIJI, PAPUA NEW GUINEA, SOLOMON ISLANDS, VANUATU, AND SAMOA
D.A. Information Services
648 Whitehorse Road
Mitcham 3132, Victoria
Tel: (61) 3 9210 7777
Fax: (61) 3 9210 7788
E-mail: service@dadirect.com.au
URL: http://www.dadirect.com.au

AUSTRIA
Gerold and Co.
Weihburggasse 26
A-1011 Wien
Tel: (43 1) 512-47-31-0
Fax: (43 1) 512-47-31-29
URL: http://www.gerold.co/at.online

BANGLADESH
Micro Industries Development Assistance Society (MIDAS)
House 5, Road 16
Dhanmondi R/Area
Dhaka 1209
Tel: (880 2) 326427
Fax: (880 2) 811188

BELGIUM
Jean De Lannoy
Av. du Roi 202
1060 Brussels
Tel: (32 2) 538-5169
Fax: (32 2) 538-0841

BRAZIL
Publicações Tecnicas Internacionais Ltda.
Rua Peixoto Gomide, 209
01409 Sao Paulo, SP.
Tel: (55 11) 259-6644
Fax: (55 11) 258-6990
E-mail: postmaster@pti.uol.br
URL: http://www.uol.br

CANADA
Renouf Publishing Co. Ltd.
5369 Canotek Road
Ottawa, Ontario K1J 9J3
Tel: (613) 745-2665
Fax: (613) 745-7660
E-mail: order.dept@renoufbooks.com
URL: http://www.renoufbooks.com

CHINA
China Financial & Economic Publishing House
8, Da Fo Si Dong Jie
Beijing
Tel: (86 10) 6401-7365
Fax: (86 10) 6401-7365

China Book Import Centre
P.O. Box 2825
Beijing

Chinese Corporation for Promotion of Humanities
52, You Fang Hu Tong,
Xuan Nei Da Jie
Beijing
Tel: (86 10) 660 72 494
Fax: (86 10) 660 72 494

COLOMBIA
Infoenlace Ltda.
Carrera 6 No. 51-21
Apartado Aereo 34270
Santafé de Bogotá, D.C.
Tel: (57 1) 285-2798
Fax: (57 1) 285-2798

COTE D'IVOIRE
Center d'Edition et de Diffusion Africaines (CEDA)
04 B.P. 541
Abidjan 04
Tel: (225) 24 6510; 24 6511
Fax: (225) 25 0567

CYPRUS
Center for Applied Research
Cyprus College
6, Diogenes Street, Engomi
P.O. Box 2006
Nicosia
Tel: (357 2) 59-0730
Fax: (357 2) 66-2051

CZECH REPUBLIC
USIS, NIS Prodejna
Havelkova 22
130 00 Prague 3
Tel: (420 2) 2423 1486
Fax: (420 2) 2423 1114
URL: http://www.nis.cz/

DENMARK
SamfundsLitteratur
Rosenoerns Allé 11
DK-1970 Frederiksberg C
Tel: (45 35) 351942
Fax: (45 35) 357822
URL: http://www.sl.cbs.dk

ECUADOR
Libri Mundi
Libreria Internacional
P.O. Box 17-01-3029
Juan Leon Mera 851
Quito
Tel: (593 2) 521-606; (593 2) 544-185
Fax: (593 2) 504-209
E-mail: librimu1@librimundi.com.ec
E-mail: librimu2@librimundi.com.ec

CODEU
Ruiz de Castilla 763, Edif. Expocolor
Primer piso, Of. #2
Quito
Tel/Fax: (593 2) 507-383; 253-091
E-mail: codeu@impsat.net.ec

EGYPT, ARAB REPUBLIC OF
Al Ahram Distribution Agency
Al Galaa Street
Cairo
Tel: (20 2) 578-6083
Fax: (20 2) 578-6833

The Middle East Observer
41, Sherif Street
Cairo
Tel: (20 2) 393-9732
Fax: (20 2) 393-9732

FINLAND
Akateeminen Kirjakauppa
P.O. Box 128
FIN-00101 Helsinki
Tel: (358 0) 121 4418
Fax: (358 0) 121-4435
E-mail: akatilaus@stockmann.fi
URL: http://www.akateeminen.com

FRANCE
Editions Eska; DBJ
48, rue Gay Lussac
75005 Paris
Tel: (33-1) 55-42-73-08
Fax: (33-1) 43-29-91-67

GERMANY
UNO-Verlag
Poppelsdorfer Allee 55
53115 Bonn
Tel: (49 228) 949020
Fax: (49 228) 217492
URL: http://www.uno-verlag.de
E-mail: unoverlag@aol.com

GHANA
Epp Books Services
P.O. Box 44
TUC
Accra
Tel: 223 21 778843
Fax: 223 21 779099

GREECE
Papasotiriou S.A.
35, Stournara Str.
106 82 Athens
Tel: (30 1) 364-1826
Fax: (30 1) 364-8254

HAITI
Culture Diffusion
5, Rue Capois
C.P. 257
Port-au-Prince
Tel: (509) 23 9260
Fax: (509) 23 4858

HONG KONG, CHINA; MACAO
Asia 2000 Ltd.
Sales & Circulation Department
302 Seabird House
22-28 Wyndham Street, Central
Hong Kong, China
Tel: (852) 2530-1409
Fax: (852) 2526-1107
E-mail: sales@asia2000.com.hk
URL: http://www.asia2000.com.hk

HUNGARY
Euro Info Service
Margitszgeti Europa Haz
H-1138 Budapest
Tel: (36 1) 350 80 24, 350 80 25
Fax: (36 1) 350 90 32
E-mail: euroinfo@mail.matav.hu

INDIA
Allied Publishers Ltd.
751 Mount Road
Madras - 600 002
Tel: (91 44) 852-3938
Fax: (91 44) 852-0649

INDONESIA
Pt. Indira Limited
Jalan Borobudur 20
P.O. Box 181
Jakarta 10320
Tel: (62 21) 390-4290
Fax: (62 21) 390-4289

IRAN
Ketab Sara Co. Publishers
Khaled Eslamboli Ave., 6th Street
Delafrooz Alley No. 8
P.O. Box 15745-733
Tehran 15117
Tel: (98 21) 8717819; 8716104
Fax: (98 21) 8712479
E-mail: ketab-sara@neda.net.ir

Kowkab Publishers
P.O. Box 19575-511
Tehran
Tel: (98 21) 258-3723
Fax: (98 21) 258-3723

IRELAND
Government Supplies Agency
Oifig an tSoláthair
4-5 Harcourt Road
Dublin 2
Tel: (353 1) 661-3111
Fax: (353 1) 475-2670

ISRAEL
Yozmot Literature Ltd.
P.O. Box 56055
3 Yohanan Hasandlar Street
Tel Aviv 61560
Tel: (972 3) 5285-397
Fax: (972 3) 5285-397

R.O.Y. International
PO Box 13056
Tel Aviv 61130
Tel: (972 3) 649 9469
Fax: (972 3) 648 6039
E-mail: royil@netvision.net.il
URL: http://www.royint.co.il

Palestinian Authority/Middle East Index Information Services
P.O.B. 19502 Jerusalem
Tel: (972 2) 6271219
Fax: (972 2) 6271634

ITALY, LIBERIA
Licosa Commissionaria Sansoni SPA
Via Duca Di Calabria, 1/1
Casella Postale 552
50125 Firenze
Tel: (39 55) 645-415
Fax: (39 55) 641-257
E-mail: licosa@ftbcc.it
URL: http://www.ftbcc.it/licosa

JAMAICA
Ian Randle Publishers Ltd.
206 Old Hope Road, Kingston 6
Tel: 876-927-2085
Fax: 876-977-0243
E-mail: irpl@colis.com

JAPAN
Eastern Book Service
3-13 Hongo 3-chome, Bunkyo-ku
Tokyo 113
Tel: (81 3) 3818-0861
Fax: (81 3) 3818-0864
E-mail: orders@svt-ebs.co.jp
URL: http://www.bekkoame.or.jp/~svt-ebs

KENYA
Africa Book Service (E.A.) Ltd.
Quaran House, Mfangano Street
P.O. Box 45245
Nairobi
Tel: (254 2) 223 641
Fax: (254 2) 330 272

Legacy Books
Loita House
Mezzanine 1
P.O. Box 68077
Nairobi
Tel: (254) 2-330853, 221426
Fax: (254) 2-330854, 561654
E-mail: Legacy@form-net.com

KOREA, REPUBLIC OF
Dayang Books Trading Co.
International Division
783-20, Pangba Bon-Dong, Socho-ku
Seoul
Tel: (82 2) 536-9555
Fax: (82 2) 536-0025
E-mail: seamap@chollian.net

Eulyoo Publishing Co., Ltd.
46-1, Susong-Dong
Jongro-Gu
Seoul
Tel: (82 2) 734-3515
Fax: (82 2) 732-9154

LEBANON
Librairie du Liban
P.O. Box 11-9232
Beirut
Tel: (961 9) 217 944
Fax: (961 9) 217 434
E-mail: hsayegh@librairie-du-liban.com.lb
URL: http://www.librairie-du-liban.com.lb

MALAYSIA
University of Malaya Cooperative Bookshop, Limited
P.O. Box 1127
Jalan Pantai Baru
59700 Kuala Lumpur
Tel: (60 3) 756-5000
Fax: (60 3) 755-4424
E-mail: umkoop@tm.net.my

MEXICO
INFOTEC
Av. San Fernando No. 37
Col. Toriello Guerra
14050 Mexico, D.F.
Tel: (52 5) 624-2800
Fax: (52 5) 624-2822
E-mail: infotec@rtn.net.mx
URL: http://rtn.net.mx

Mundi-Prensa Mexico S.A. de C.V.
c/Rio Panuco, 141-Colonia Cuauhtemoc
06500 Mexico, D.F.
Tel: (52 5) 533-5658
Fax: (52 5) 514-6799

NEPAL
Everest Media International Services (P.) Ltd.
GPO Box 5443
Kathmandu
Tel: (977 1) 416 026
Fax: (977 1) 224 431

NETHERLANDS
De Lindeboom/Internationale Publicaties b.v.-
P.O. Box 202, 7480 AE Haaksbergen
Tel: (31 53) 574-0004
Fax: (31 53) 572-9296
E-mail: lindeboo@worldonline.nl
URL: http://www.worldonline.nl/~lindeboo

NEW ZEALAND
EBSCO NZ Ltd.
Private Mail Bag 99914
New Market
Auckland
Tel: (64 9) 524-8119
Fax: (64 9) 524-8067

Oasis Official
P.O. Box 3627
Wellington
Tel: (64 4) 499 1551
Fax: (64 4) 499 1972
E-mail: oasis@actrix.gen.nz
URL: http://www.oasisbooks.co.nz/

NIGERIA
University Press Limited
Three Crowns Building Jericho
Private Mail Bag 5095
Ibadan
Tel: (234 22) 41-1356
Fax: (234 22) 41-2056

PAKISTAN
Mirza Book Agency
65, Shahrah-e-Quaid-e-Azam
Lahore 54000
Tel: (92 42) 735 3601
Fax: (92 42) 576 3714

Oxford University Press
5 Bangalore Town
Sharae Faisal
PO Box 13033
Karachi-75350
Tel: (92 21) 446307
Fax: (92 21) 4547640
E-mail: ouppak@TheOffice.net

Pak Book Corporation
Aziz Chambers 21, Queen's Road
Lahore
Tel: (92 42) 636 3222; 636 0885
Fax: (92 42) 636 2328
E-mail: pbc@brain.net.pk

PERU
Editorial Desarrollo SA
Apartado 3824, Ica 242 OF. 106
Lima 1
Tel: (51 14) 285380
Fax: (51 14) 286628

PHILIPPINES
International Booksource Center Inc.
1127-A Antipolo St, Barangay, Venezuela
Makati City
Tel: (63 2) 896 6501; 6505; 6507
Fax: (63 2) 896 1741

POLAND
International Publishing Service
Ul. Piekna 31/37
00-677 Warzawa
Tel: (48 2) 628-6089
Fax: (48 2) 621-7255
E-mail: books%ips@ikp.atm.com.pl
URL: http://www.ipscg.waw.pl/ips/export

PORTUGAL
Livraria Portugal
Apartado 2681, Rua Do Carm o 70-74
1200 Lisbon
Tel: (1) 347-4982
Fax: (1) 347-0264

ROMANIA
Compani De Librarii Bucuresti S.A.
Str. Lipscani no. 26, sector 3
Bucharest
Tel: (40 1) 313 9645
Fax: (40 1) 312 4000

RUSSIAN FEDERATION
Isdatelstvo <Ves Mir>
9a, Kolpachniy Pereulok
Moscow 101831
Tel: (7 095) 917 87 49
Fax: (7 095) 917 92 59
ozimarin@glasnet.ru

SINGAPORE; TAIWAN, CHINA MYANMAR; BRUNEI
Hemisphere Publication Services
41 Kallang Pudding Road #04-03
Golden Wheel Building
Singapore 349316
Tel: (65) 741-5166
Fax: (65) 742-9356
E-mail: ashgate@asianconnect.com

SLOVENIA
Gospodarski vestnik Publishing Group
Dunajska cesta 5
1000 Ljubljana
Tel: (386 61) 133 83 47; 132 12 30
Fax: (386 61) 133 80 30
E-mail: repansekj@gvestnik.si

SOUTH AFRICA, BOTSWANA
For single titles:
Oxford University Press Southern Africa
Vasco Boulevard, Goodwood
P.O. Box 12119, N1 City 7463
Cape Town
Tel: (27 21) 595 4400
Fax: (27 21) 595 4430
E-mail: oxford@oup.co.za

For subscription orders:
International Subscription Service
P.O. Box 41095
Craighall
Johannesburg 2024
Tel: (27 11) 880-1448
Fax: (27 11) 880-6248
E-mail: iss@is.co.za

SPAIN
Mundi-Prensa Libros, S.A.
Castello 37
28001 Madrid
Tel: (34 91) 4 363700
Fax: (34 91) 5 753998
E-mail: liberia@mundiprensa.es
URL: http://www.mundiprensa.com/

Mundi-Prensa Barcelona
Consell de Cent, 391
08009 Barcelona
Tel: (34 3) 488-3492
Fax: (34 3) 487-7659
E-mail: barcelona@mundiprensa.es

SRI LANKA, THE MALDIVES
Lake House Bookshop
100, Sir Chittampalam Gardiner Mawatha
Colombo 2
Tel: (94 1) 32105
Fax: (94 1) 432104
E-mail: LHL@sri.lanka.net

SWEDEN
Wennergren-Williams AB
P. O. Box 1305
S-171 25 Solna
Tel: (46 8) 705-97-50
Fax: (46 8) 27-00-71
E-mail: mail@wwi.se

SWITZERLAND
Librairie Payot Service Institutionnel
C(tm)tes-de-Montbenon 30
1002 Lausanne
Tel: (41 21) 341-3229
Fax: (41 21) 341-3235

ADECO Van Diermen EditionsTechniques
Ch. de Lacuez 41
CH1807 Blonay
Tel: (41 21) 943 2673
Fax: (41 21) 943 3605

THAILAND
Central Books Distribution
306 Silom Road
Bangkok 10500
Tel: (66 2) 2336930-9
Fax: (66 2) 237-8321

TRINIDAD & TOBAGO AND THE CARRIBBEAN
Systematics Studies Ltd.
St. Augustine Shopping Center
Eastern Main Road, St. Augustine
Trinidad & Tobago, West Indies
Tel: (868) 645-8466
Fax: (868) 645-8467
E-mail: tobe@trinidad.net

UGANDA
Gustro Ltd.
PO Box 9997, Madhvani Building
Plot 16/4 Jinja Rd.
Kampala
Tel: (256 41) 251 467
Fax: (256 41) 251 468
E-mail: gus@swiftuganda.com

UNITED KINGDOM
Microinfo Ltd.
P.O. Box 3, Omega Park, Alton, Hampshire GU34 2PG
England
Tel: (44 1420) 86848
Fax: (44 1420) 89889
E-mail: wbank@microinfo.co.uk
URL: http://www.microinfo.co.uk

The Stationery Office
51 Nine Elms Lane
London SW8 5DR
Tel: (44 171) 873-8400
Fax: (44 171) 873-8242
URL: http://www.the-stationery-office.co.uk/

VENEZUELA
Tecni-Ciencia Libros, S.A.
Centro Cuidad Comercial Tamanco
Nivel C2, Caracas
Tel: (58 2) 959 5547; 5035; 0016
Fax: (58 2) 959 5636

ZAMBIA
University Bookshop, University of Zambia
Great East Road Campus
P.O. Box 32379
Lusaka
Tel: (260 1) 252 576
Fax: (260 1) 253 952

ZIMBABWE
Academic and Baobab Books (Pvt.) Ltd.
4 Conald Road, Graniteside
P.O. Box 567
Harare
Tel: 263 4 755035
Fax: 263 4 781913